THE 5 SECOND JOURNAL

THE FASTEST WAY TO SLOW DOWN, POWER UP, AND GET SH*T DONE!

IF FOUND, TAKE 5 SECONDS TO RETURN TO:

NAME:

....

PHONE:

....

THE CONFIDENCE PROJECT PRESS

BOSTON, MASSACHUSETTS

PUBLISHED IN THE USA

PRINTED IN CHINA

A CONFIDENCE PROJECT PRESS BOOK

ISBN: 978-1-68261-722-9

THE 5 SECOND JOURNAL © *2017*

ALL RIGHTS RESERVED

COVER & INTERIOR DESIGN

By Rockstar Design Duo: Rachel Greenberg & Robin Garstka

RESEARCH PHENOM

Tracey Merz

THIRD PRINTING

FOR MORE INFORMATION: www.5SecondJournal.com

5 SECOND JOURNAL

FOR YOU

For a long time, I was the kind of person who was busy but not productive. I was a professional to-do list maker. I bought planners and highlighters because they made me feel like I was getting my life together. But there was a problem. Despite how hard I worked, I could never find time for the important stuff.

After years of spinning in circles, I finally found my saving grace—science.

What started as a research project quickly turned into an obsession, as I discovered amazing productivity, happiness, and confidence hacks. When I started applying these proven strategies in my own life and work, the difference was immediate.

Now I want to share them with you. Inside these pages, you'll learn a simple, research-backed journaling method that will give you control over your day, your time, and your future.

So crack this open with a fiery spirit, big goals, and an open mind.

You're about to learn how to
5-4-3-2-1 ... GET SH*T DONE.

THE MOST POWERFUL JOURNAL ON THE PLANET

Using science, this journal will unlock the most powerful force in the Universe ... YOU.

Right now, you are holding yourself back and you don't even know it. The **5 Second Journal** will show you the simplest way to take back control and make progress on things that matter. The result? That sense of pride, passion, and confidence in yourself that feels so damn amazing.

To learn more about the research, the methodology and case studies, check out www.5secondjournal.com.

✓ GET SH*T DONE

You won't just get more done—you'll do it in half the time. Your life is way too important to spend it procrastinating. Invest a little time in here every day and in return you'll get the best tools psychology, organizational behavioral, and neuroscience have to offer.

👄 KISS OVERWHELM GOODBYE

Stop being ruled by your to-do list and start getting the important work done. Filling your days with menial tasks will not lead to a meaningful life. This journal will keep your focus on what's most important, even in between conference calls and running errands.

☝ CULTIVATE ROCKSTAR CONFIDENCE

Confidence is a skill YOU can build. Yes, you. And it's not as difficult as you may think. Every day this journal will push you forward, to step outside your comfort zone so you can feel proud of yourself and watch your self-confidence grow.

❤ AMP YOUR PASSION

Want to live a more passionate life? Stop focusing on sh*t that drains you. Seriously. This journal will show you a cool way to power up your energy levels and tap into that inner zen that knows exactly what fuels your fire.

🎯 GET CONTROL OF YOUR LIFE

If you get to the end of the day and wonder where it all went, it's time to take stock. Using research from Harvard Business School, you'll learn one simple mindset trick that keeps you present to what matters most, which is the secret to being in control.

☺ BE THE HAPPIEST YOU

Science proves that your mood in the morning impacts your entire day. That's why this journal is designed to boost your mood first thing, so you can become a happier, smarter, and more positive person all day. The fact is, happier people get sh*t done.

1

Record the time and place, and years from now you'll remember this moment.

2

Assess your energy level to get present.

3

Describe your energy level to gain clarity.

4

Commit to something that energizes you to power up and unlock the passion inside of you.

5

Before your day gets hijacked, put yourself first by describing your top project for the day.

6

Give your commitment to action a boost by describing why this project matters to you.

7

Harvard researchers say one small move forward taps the "Progress Principle" to boost happiness.

8

Use this space for anything else you wish to include in your daily planning.

9

To tap the power of gratitude, savor one thing about this moment.

10

Give your work a deadline, then plan backwards to increase productivity and guarantee life balance.

⏱ TIME 7:15am   📍 PLACE Clever Monk Coffee Shop   DATE 10/6

TODAY I FEEL
(C'MON. BE HONEST)

I FEEL THIS WAY BECAUSE ...
- I woke up feeling tired
- I've got a lot going on at wor
- Didn't exercise yesterday

TO FEEL MORE ENERGIZED I CAN ...
(WHAT PEOPLE OR ACTIVITIES GIVE YOU A BOOST?)

I can have lunch with Sarah and sign up for a 6pm spin class after work. I can also tidy up the kitchen before I leave for the day.

TODAY, MY TOP PROJECT IS ...

Publishing my first novel inspired by my grandmother's remarkable life that I've been wanting to write for years.

THIS PROJECT MATTERS TO ME BECAUSE ...
- I hate my job and I've always dreamt of being a writer and working on it will help me stop thinking and get started.

ONE SMALL ACTION I CAN TAKE TO MOVE FORWARD IS ...
- Google 'self-publishing advice' and watch two video tutorials the topic. Take notes.

OTHER THOUGHTS ...

TODAY, I'M GRATEFUL FOR ...

My dog, Molly, she's sitting here at my feet right now.

TODAY, I WILL STOP WORKING AT ...

5:30   AM PM

THE BEST DAY EVER

☀

6:00   5 Second Daily Journal

7:00
        MEETING NOTES:

8:00   commute—call mom
        • Launch Date: May 8th – have
          new site up by April 6th. Work with
9:00   plan work day
          Troy on content and have ready to
          roll by Feb 15th.

10:00
        • Arrange flights for April. Work with
10:30 make sales calls
          travel agency to confirlm hotel and car
11:00
          schedules.

        • Contact printer to confirm delivery
12:00 lunch with sarah
          dates for January 31st.
        • Plan follow-up meeting.

1:00

2:00   finish ppt

3:00

4:00   meeting with team
        ! TOP DAILY TO DOs:
          • Pay credit card
5:00
          • Change Netflix password
5:30   stop working
          • Gym membership
6:00

7:00   spin class

8:00   Time to hang! ☺

☾
▲
You're awesome! Go rock the day!

11

Every day is different and that's why this page is designed to be flexible to meet your needs.

12

Use this page to journal, take notes or brain dump your to do list and important ideas. It's your space to get the most out of your day.

13

This handy timeline can be used to plan and organize your day.

5-4-3-2-1

GET SH*T DONE!

·················►

TODAY I FEEL
(C'MON, BE HONEST - CIRCLE ONE)

I FEEL THIS WAY BECAUSE ...

-
-
-

TO FEEL MORE ENERGIZED I CAN ...
(WHAT PEOPLE OR ACTIVITIES GIVE YOU A BOOST?)

_____

_____

TODAY, MY TOP PROJECT IS ...

_____

_____

THIS PROJECT MATTERS TO ME BECAUSE ...

-

ONE SMALL ACTION I CAN TAKE TO MOVE FORWARD IS ...

-

OTHER THOUGHTS ...

_____

_____

_____

_____

_____

TODAY, I'M GRATEFUL FOR ...

_____

TODAY, I WILL STOP WORKING AT ...

_____ AM / PM

NOTES — PLAN THE DAY — BRAIN DUMP
(FREE SPACE TO HELP FREE YOUR MIND)

☀

6:00

7:00

8:00

9:00

10:00

11:00

12:00

1:00

2:00

3:00

4:00

5:00

6:00

7:00

8:00

☾

You're awesome! Go rock the day! 😌 👍 🚀 💥

TODAY I FEEL
(C'MON, BE HONEST - CIRCLE ONE)

I FEEL THIS WAY BECAUSE ...

-
-
-

TO FEEL MORE ENERGIZED I CAN ...
(WHAT PEOPLE OR ACTIVITIES GIVE YOU A BOOST?)

TODAY, MY TOP PROJECT IS ...

THIS PROJECT MATTERS TO ME BECAUSE ...

-

ONE SMALL ACTION I CAN TAKE TO MOVE FORWARD IS ...

-

OTHER THOUGHTS ...

TODAY, I'M GRATEFUL FOR ...

TODAY, I WILL STOP WORKING AT ...

_____ AM / PM

NOTES — PLAN THE DAY — BRAIN DUMP
(FREE SPACE TO HELP FREE YOUR MIND)

☀

6:00

7:00

8:00

9:00

10:00

11:00

12:00

1:00

2:00

3:00

4:00

5:00

6:00

7:00

8:00

☾

You're awesome! Go rock the day! 😄 👍 🚀 💥

TODAY I FEEL
(C'MON, BE HONEST - CIRCLE ONE)

I FEEL THIS WAY BECAUSE ...

-
-
-

TO FEEL MORE ENERGIZED I CAN ...
(WHAT PEOPLE OR ACTIVITIES GIVE YOU A BOOST?)

TODAY, MY TOP PROJECT IS ...

THIS PROJECT MATTERS TO ME BECAUSE ...

-

ONE SMALL ACTION I CAN TAKE TO MOVE FORWARD IS ...

-

OTHER THOUGHTS ...

TODAY, I'M GRATEFUL FOR ...

TODAY, I WILL STOP WORKING AT ...

_____ AM / PM

NOTES — PLAN THE DAY — BRAIN DUMP

(FREE SPACE TO HELP FREE YOUR MIND)

☀

6:00

7:00

8:00

9:00

10:00

11:00

12:00

1:00

2:00

3:00

4:00

5:00

6:00

7:00

8:00

☾

You're awesome! Go rock the day! 😉 👍 🚀 💥

TODAY I FEEL
(C'MON, BE HONEST - CIRCLE ONE)

I FEEL THIS WAY BECAUSE …

-
-
-

TO FEEL MORE ENERGIZED I CAN …
(WHAT PEOPLE OR ACTIVITIES GIVE YOU A BOOST?)

TODAY, MY TOP PROJECT IS …

THIS PROJECT MATTERS TO ME BECAUSE …

-

ONE SMALL ACTION I CAN TAKE TO MOVE FORWARD IS …

-

OTHER THOUGHTS …

TODAY, I'M GRATEFUL FOR …

TODAY, I WILL STOP WORKING AT …

_____ AM / PM

☀

6:00

7:00

8:00

9:00

10:00

11:00

12:00

1:00

2:00

3:00

4:00

5:00

6:00

7:00

8:00

☾

You're awesome! Go rock the day! 😊 👍 🚀 💥

TODAY I FEEL
(C'MON, BE HONEST - CIRCLE ONE)

I FEEL THIS WAY BECAUSE ...

-
-
-

TO FEEL MORE ENERGIZED I CAN ...
(WHAT PEOPLE OR ACTIVITIES GIVE YOU A BOOST?)

TODAY, MY TOP PROJECT IS ...

THIS PROJECT MATTERS TO ME BECAUSE ...

-

ONE SMALL ACTION I CAN TAKE TO MOVE FORWARD IS ...

-

OTHER THOUGHTS ...

TODAY, I'M GRATEFUL FOR ...

TODAY, I WILL STOP WORKING AT ...

_____ AM / PM

NOTES — PLAN THE DAY — BRAIN DUMP
(FREE SPACE TO HELP FREE YOUR MIND)

☀

6:00

7:00

8:00

9:00

10:00

11:00

12:00

1:00

2:00

3:00

4:00

5:00

6:00

7:00

8:00

☾

You're awesome! Go rock the day! 😌 👍 🚀 💥

TODAY I FEEL
(C'MON, BE HONEST - CIRCLE ONE)

I FEEL THIS WAY BECAUSE ...

-
-
-

TO FEEL MORE ENERGIZED I CAN ...
(WHAT PEOPLE OR ACTIVITIES GIVE YOU A BOOST?)

TODAY, MY TOP PROJECT IS ...

THIS PROJECT MATTERS TO ME BECAUSE ...

-

ONE SMALL ACTION I CAN TAKE TO MOVE FORWARD IS ...

-

OTHER THOUGHTS ...

TODAY, I'M GRATEFUL FOR ...

TODAY, I WILL STOP WORKING AT ...

_____ AM / PM

☀

6:00

7:00

8:00

9:00

10:00

11:00

12:00

1:00

2:00

3:00

4:00

5:00

6:00

7:00

8:00

☾

You're awesome! Go rock the day! 😊👍🚀💥

TODAY I FEEL
(C'MON, BE HONEST - CIRCLE ONE)

I FEEL THIS WAY BECAUSE ...

-
-
-

TO FEEL MORE ENERGIZED I CAN ...
(WHAT PEOPLE OR ACTIVITIES GIVE YOU A BOOST?)

_____

_____

TODAY, MY TOP PROJECT IS ...

_____

_____

THIS PROJECT MATTERS TO ME BECAUSE ...

-

ONE SMALL ACTION I CAN TAKE TO MOVE FORWARD IS ...

-

OTHER THOUGHTS ...

_____

_____

_____

_____

_____

TODAY, I'M GRATEFUL FOR ...

_____

TODAY, I WILL STOP WORKING AT ...

_____ AM / PM

☀

6:00

7:00

8:00

9:00

10:00

11:00

12:00

1:00

2:00

3:00

4:00

5:00

6:00

7:00

8:00

☾

You're awesome! Go rock the day! 😊 👍 🚀 💥

TODY I FEEL

TODAY I FEEL
(C'MON, BE HONEST - CIRCLE ONE)

I FEEL THIS WAY BECAUSE ...

-
-
-

TO FEEL MORE ENERGIZED I CAN ...
(WHAT PEOPLE OR ACTIVITIES GIVE YOU A BOOST?)

TODAY, MY TOP PROJECT IS ...

THIS PROJECT MATTERS TO ME BECAUSE ...

-

ONE SMALL ACTION I CAN TAKE TO MOVE FORWARD IS ...

-

OTHER THOUGHTS ...

TODAY, I'M GRATEFUL FOR ...

TODAY, I WILL STOP WORKING AT ...

_____ AM / PM

NOTES — PLAN THE DAY — BRAIN DUMP
(FREE SPACE TO HELP FREE YOUR MIND)

☀

6:00

7:00

8:00

9:00

10:00

11:00

12:00

1:00

2:00

3:00

4:00

5:00

6:00

7:00

8:00

☾

You're awesome! Go rock the day! 😉 👍 🚀 💥

TODAY I FEEL
(C'MON, BE HONEST - CIRCLE ONE)

I FEEL THIS WAY BECAUSE ...

-
-
-

TO FEEL MORE ENERGIZED I CAN ...
(WHAT PEOPLE OR ACTIVITIES GIVE YOU A BOOST?)

TODAY, MY TOP PROJECT IS ...

THIS PROJECT MATTERS TO ME BECAUSE ...

-

ONE SMALL ACTION I CAN TAKE TO MOVE FORWARD IS ...

-

OTHER THOUGHTS ...

TODAY, I'M GRATEFUL FOR ...

TODAY, I WILL STOP WORKING AT ...

_____ AM / PM

☀

6:00

7:00

8:00

9:00

10:00

11:00

12:00

1:00

2:00

3:00

4:00

5:00

6:00

7:00

8:00

☾

You're awesome! Go rock the day! 😜 👍 🚀 💥

TODAY I FEEL
(C'MON, BE HONEST - CIRCLE ONE)

I FEEL THIS WAY BECAUSE ...

-
-
-

TO FEEL MORE ENERGIZED I CAN ...
(WHAT PEOPLE OR ACTIVITIES GIVE YOU A BOOST?)

_____

_____

TODAY, MY TOP PROJECT IS ...

_____

THIS PROJECT MATTERS TO ME BECAUSE ...

-

ONE SMALL ACTION I CAN TAKE TO MOVE FORWARD IS ...

-

OTHER THOUGHTS ...

_____
_____
_____
_____
_____

TODAY, I'M GRATEFUL FOR ...

_____

TODAY, I WILL STOP WORKING AT ...

_____ AM / PM

☀

6:00

7:00

8:00

9:00

10:00

11:00

12:00

1:00

2:00

3:00

4:00

5:00

6:00

7:00

8:00

☾

You're awesome! Go rock the day! 😉 👍 🚀 💥

TODAY I FEEL
(C'MON, BE HONEST - CIRCLE ONE)

I FEEL THIS WAY BECAUSE ...

-
-
-

TO FEEL MORE ENERGIZED I CAN ...
(WHAT PEOPLE OR ACTIVITIES GIVE YOU A BOOST?)

TODAY, MY TOP PROJECT IS ...

THIS PROJECT MATTERS TO ME BECAUSE ...

-

ONE SMALL ACTION I CAN TAKE TO MOVE FORWARD IS ...

-

OTHER THOUGHTS ...

TODAY, I'M GRATEFUL FOR ...

TODAY, I WILL STOP WORKING AT ...

_____ AM / PM

NOTES — PLAN THE DAY — BRAIN DUMP
(FREE SPACE TO HELP FREE YOUR MIND)

☀

6:00

7:00

8:00

9:00

10:00

11:00

12:00

1:00

2:00

3:00

4:00

5:00

6:00

7:00

8:00

☾

You're awesome! Go rock the day! 😊 👍 🚀 💥

TODAY I FEEL
(C'MON, BE HONEST - CIRCLE ONE)

I FEEL THIS WAY BECAUSE ...

-
-
-

TO FEEL MORE ENERGIZED I CAN ...
(WHAT PEOPLE OR ACTIVITIES GIVE YOU A BOOST?)

_____

TODAY, MY TOP PROJECT IS ...

_____

THIS PROJECT MATTERS TO ME BECAUSE ...

-

ONE SMALL ACTION I CAN TAKE TO MOVE FORWARD IS ...

-

OTHER THOUGHTS ...

_____
_____
_____
_____
_____

TODAY, I'M GRATEFUL FOR ...

_____
_____

TODAY, I WILL STOP WORKING AT ...

_____ AM / PM

NOTES — PLAN THE DAY — BRAIN DUMP
(FREE SPACE TO HELP FREE YOUR MIND)

☀

6:00

7:00

8:00

9:00

10:00

11:00

12:00

1:00

2:00

3:00

4:00

5:00

6:00

7:00

8:00

☾

You're awesome! Go rock the day! 😉 👍 🚀 💥

TODAY I FEEL

(C'MON, BE HONEST - CIRCLE ONE)

I FEEL THIS WAY BECAUSE ...

-
-
-

TO FEEL MORE ENERGIZED I CAN ...

(WHAT PEOPLE OR ACTIVITIES GIVE YOU A BOOST?)

TODAY, MY TOP PROJECT IS ...

THIS PROJECT MATTERS TO ME BECAUSE ...

-

ONE SMALL ACTION I CAN TAKE TO MOVE FORWARD IS ...

-

OTHER THOUGHTS ...

TODAY, I'M GRATEFUL FOR ...

TODAY, I WILL STOP WORKING AT ...

_____ AM / PM

34

☀

6:00

7:00

8:00

9:00

10:00

11:00

12:00

1:00

2:00

3:00

4:00

5:00

6:00

7:00

8:00

☾

You're awesome! Go rock the day! 😊 👍 🚀 💥

TODAY I FEEL
(C'MON, BE HONEST - CIRCLE ONE)

I FEEL THIS WAY BECAUSE ...

-
-
-

TO FEEL MORE ENERGIZED I CAN ...
(WHAT PEOPLE OR ACTIVITIES GIVE YOU A BOOST?)

TODAY, MY TOP PROJECT IS ...

THIS PROJECT MATTERS TO ME BECAUSE ...

-

ONE SMALL ACTION I CAN TAKE TO MOVE FORWARD IS ...

-

OTHER THOUGHTS ...

TODAY, I'M GRATEFUL FOR ...

TODAY, I WILL STOP WORKING AT ...

_____ AM / PM

☀

6:00

7:00

8:00

9:00

10:00

11:00

12:00

1:00

2:00

3:00

4:00

5:00

6:00

7:00

8:00

☾

You're awesome! Go rock the day! 😌 👍 🚀 💥

TODAY I FEEL
(C'MON, BE HONEST - CIRCLE ONE)

I FEEL THIS WAY BECAUSE ...

-
-
-

TO FEEL MORE ENERGIZED I CAN ...
(WHAT PEOPLE OR ACTIVITIES GIVE YOU A BOOST?)

TODAY, MY TOP PROJECT IS ...

THIS PROJECT MATTERS TO ME BECAUSE ...

-

ONE SMALL ACTION I CAN TAKE TO MOVE FORWARD IS ...

-

OTHER THOUGHTS ...

TODAY, I'M GRATEFUL FOR ...

TODAY, I WILL STOP WORKING AT ...

_____ AM / PM

☀

6:00

7:00

8:00

9:00

10:00

11:00

12:00

1:00

2:00

3:00

4:00

5:00

6:00

7:00

8:00

☾

You're awesome! Go rock the day! 😊 👍 🚀 💥

TODAY I FEEL
(C'MON, BE HONEST - CIRCLE ONE)

I FEEL THIS WAY BECAUSE ...

-
-
-

TO FEEL MORE ENERGIZED I CAN ...
(WHAT PEOPLE OR ACTIVITIES GIVE YOU A BOOST?)

_____

_____

TODAY, MY TOP PROJECT IS ...

_____

_____

THIS PROJECT MATTERS TO ME BECAUSE ...

-

ONE SMALL ACTION I CAN TAKE TO MOVE FORWARD IS ...

-

OTHER THOUGHTS ...

_____
_____
_____
_____
_____

TODAY, I'M GRATEFUL FOR ...

_____
_____

TODAY, I WILL STOP WORKING AT ...

_____ AM / PM

NOTES — PLAN THE DAY — BRAIN DUMP

(FREE SPACE TO HELP FREE YOUR MIND)

☀

6:00

7:00

8:00

9:00

10:00

11:00

12:00

1:00

2:00

3:00

4:00

5:00

6:00

7:00

8:00

☾

You're awesome! Go rock the day! 😴 👍 🚀 💥

TODAY I FEEL
(C'MON, BE HONEST - CIRCLE ONE)

I FEEL THIS WAY BECAUSE ...

-
-
-

TO FEEL MORE ENERGIZED I CAN ...
(WHAT PEOPLE OR ACTIVITIES GIVE YOU A BOOST?)

TODAY, MY TOP PROJECT IS ...

THIS PROJECT MATTERS TO ME BECAUSE ...

-

ONE SMALL ACTION I CAN TAKE TO MOVE FORWARD IS ...

-

OTHER THOUGHTS ...

TODAY, I'M GRATEFUL FOR ...

TODAY, I WILL STOP WORKING AT ...

_____ AM / PM

NOTES — PLAN THE DAY — BRAIN DUMP

(FREE SPACE TO HELP FREE YOUR MIND)

☀

6:00

7:00

8:00

9:00

10:00

11:00

12:00

1:00

2:00

3:00

4:00

5:00

6:00

7:00

8:00

☾

You're awesome! Go rock the day! 😉👍🚀💥

TODAY I FEEL
(C'MON, BE HONEST - CIRCLE ONE)

I FEEL THIS WAY BECAUSE ...

-
-
-

TO FEEL MORE ENERGIZED I CAN ...
(WHAT PEOPLE OR ACTIVITIES GIVE YOU A BOOST?)

_____

_____

TODAY, MY TOP PROJECT IS ...

_____

_____

THIS PROJECT MATTERS TO ME BECAUSE ...

-

ONE SMALL ACTION I CAN TAKE TO MOVE FORWARD IS ...

-

OTHER THOUGHTS ...

_____

_____

_____

_____

_____

TODAY, I'M GRATEFUL FOR ...

TODAY, I WILL STOP WORKING AT ...

_____ AM / PM

☀

6:00

7:00

8:00

9:00

10:00

11:00

12:00

1:00

2:00

3:00

4:00

5:00

6:00

7:00

8:00

☾

You're awesome! Go rock the day! 😊 👍 🚀 💥

TODAY I FEEL

(C'MON, BE HONEST - CIRCLE ONE)

I FEEL THIS WAY BECAUSE ...

-
-
-

TO FEEL MORE ENERGIZED I CAN ...
(WHAT PEOPLE OR ACTIVITIES GIVE YOU A BOOST?)

TODAY, MY TOP PROJECT IS ...

THIS PROJECT MATTERS TO ME BECAUSE ...

-

ONE SMALL ACTION I CAN TAKE TO MOVE FORWARD IS ...

-

OTHER THOUGHTS ...

TODAY, I'M GRATEFUL FOR ...

TODAY, I WILL STOP WORKING AT ...

_____ AM / PM

☀

6:00

7:00

8:00

9:00

10:00

11:00

12:00

1:00

2:00

3:00

4:00

5:00

6:00

7:00

8:00

☾

You're awesome! Go rock the day! 😊 👍 🚀 💥

TODAY I FEEL
(C'MON, BE HONEST - CIRCLE ONE)

I FEEL THIS WAY BECAUSE ...

-
-
-

TO FEEL MORE ENERGIZED I CAN ...
(WHAT PEOPLE OR ACTIVITIES GIVE YOU A BOOST?)

TODAY, MY TOP PROJECT IS ...

THIS PROJECT MATTERS TO ME BECAUSE ...

-

ONE SMALL ACTION I CAN TAKE TO MOVE FORWARD IS ...

-

OTHER THOUGHTS ...

TODAY, I'M GRATEFUL FOR ...

TODAY, I WILL STOP WORKING AT ...

_____ AM / PM

NOTES — PLAN THE DAY — BRAIN DUMP

(FREE SPACE TO HELP FREE YOUR MIND)

☀

6:00

7:00

8:00

9:00

10:00

11:00

12:00

1:00

2:00

3:00

4:00

5:00

6:00

7:00

8:00

☾

You're awesome! Go rock the day! 😉 👍 🚀 💥

TODAY I FEEL
(C'MON, BE HONEST - CIRCLE ONE)

I FEEL THIS WAY BECAUSE ...

-
-
-

TO FEEL MORE ENERGIZED I CAN ...
(WHAT PEOPLE OR ACTIVITIES GIVE YOU A BOOST?)

TODAY, MY TOP PROJECT IS ...

THIS PROJECT MATTERS TO ME BECAUSE ...

-

ONE SMALL ACTION I CAN TAKE TO MOVE FORWARD IS ...

-

OTHER THOUGHTS ...

TODAY, I'M GRATEFUL FOR ...

TODAY, I WILL STOP WORKING AT ...

_____ AM / PM

☀

6:00

7:00

8:00

9:00

10:00

11:00

12:00

1:00

2:00

3:00

4:00

5:00

6:00

7:00

8:00

☾

You're awesome! Go rock the day! 😊 👍 🚀 💥

TODAY I FEEL
(C'MON, BE HONEST - CIRCLE ONE)

I FEEL THIS WAY BECAUSE ...

-
-
-

TO FEEL MORE ENERGIZED I CAN ...
(WHAT PEOPLE OR ACTIVITIES GIVE YOU A BOOST?)

TODAY, MY TOP PROJECT IS ...

THIS PROJECT MATTERS TO ME BECAUSE ...

-

ONE SMALL ACTION I CAN TAKE TO MOVE FORWARD IS ...

-

OTHER THOUGHTS ...

TODAY, I'M GRATEFUL FOR ...

TODAY, I WILL STOP WORKING AT ...

_____ AM / PM

NOTES — PLAN THE DAY — BRAIN DUMP
(FREE SPACE TO HELP FREE YOUR MIND)

☀

6:00

7:00

8:00

9:00

10:00

11:00

12:00

1:00

2:00

3:00

4:00

5:00

6:00

7:00

8:00

☾

You're awesome! Go rock the day! 😊 👍 🚀 💥

TIME   PLACE   DATE

TODAY I FEEL
(C'MON, BE HONEST - CIRCLE ONE)

I FEEL THIS WAY BECAUSE …

-
-
-

TO FEEL MORE ENERGIZED I CAN …
(WHAT PEOPLE OR ACTIVITIES GIVE YOU A BOOST?)

TODAY, MY TOP PROJECT IS …

THIS PROJECT MATTERS TO ME BECAUSE …

-

ONE SMALL ACTION I CAN TAKE TO MOVE FORWARD IS …

-

OTHER THOUGHTS …

TODAY, I'M GRATEFUL FOR …

TODAY, I WILL STOP WORKING AT …

_____ AM / PM

☀

6:00

7:00

8:00

9:00

10:00

11:00

12:00

1:00

2:00

3:00

4:00

5:00

6:00

7:00

8:00

☾

You're awesome! Go rock the day! 😊 👍 🚀 💥

TODAY I FEEL
(C'MON, BE HONEST - CIRCLE ONE)

I FEEL THIS WAY BECAUSE …

-
-
-

TO FEEL MORE ENERGIZED I CAN …
(WHAT PEOPLE OR ACTIVITIES GIVE YOU A BOOST?)

TODAY, MY TOP PROJECT IS …

THIS PROJECT MATTERS TO ME BECAUSE …

-

ONE SMALL ACTION I CAN TAKE TO MOVE FORWARD IS …

-

OTHER THOUGHTS …

TODAY, I'M GRATEFUL FOR …

TODAY, I WILL STOP WORKING AT …

_____ AM / PM

☀

6:00

7:00

8:00

9:00

10:00

11:00

12:00

1:00

2:00

3:00

4:00

5:00

6:00

7:00

8:00

☾

You're awesome! Go rock the day! 😉 👍 🚀 💥

TODAY I FEEL
(C'MON, BE HONEST - CIRCLE ONE)

I FEEL THIS WAY BECAUSE ...

-
-
-

TO FEEL MORE ENERGIZED I CAN ...
(WHAT PEOPLE OR ACTIVITIES GIVE YOU A BOOST?)

TODAY, MY TOP PROJECT IS ...

THIS PROJECT MATTERS TO ME BECAUSE ...

-

ONE SMALL ACTION I CAN TAKE TO MOVE FORWARD IS ...

-

OTHER THOUGHTS ...

TODAY, I'M GRATEFUL FOR ...

TODAY, I WILL STOP WORKING AT ...

_____ AM / PM

☀

6:00

7:00

8:00

9:00

10:00

11:00

12:00

1:00

2:00

3:00

4:00

5:00

6:00

7:00

8:00

☾

You're awesome! Go rock the day! 😌 👍 🚀 💥

TODAY I FEEL
(C'MON, BE HONEST - CIRCLE ONE)

I FEEL THIS WAY BECAUSE ...

-
-
-

TO FEEL MORE ENERGIZED I CAN ...
(WHAT PEOPLE OR ACTIVITIES GIVE YOU A BOOST?)

_____

TODAY, MY TOP PROJECT IS ...

_____

THIS PROJECT MATTERS TO ME BECAUSE ...

-

ONE SMALL ACTION I CAN TAKE TO MOVE FORWARD IS ...

-

OTHER THOUGHTS ...

_____

TODAY, I'M GRATEFUL FOR ...

_____

TODAY, I WILL STOP WORKING AT ...

_____ AM / PM

☀

6:00

7:00

8:00

9:00

10:00

11:00

12:00

1:00

2:00

3:00

4:00

5:00

6:00

7:00

8:00

☾

You're awesome! Go rock the day! 😊 👍 🚀 💥

TODAY I FEEL
(C'MON, BE HONEST - CIRCLE ONE)

I FEEL THIS WAY BECAUSE ...

-
-
-

TO FEEL MORE ENERGIZED I CAN ...
(WHAT PEOPLE OR ACTIVITIES GIVE YOU A BOOST?)

TODAY, MY TOP PROJECT IS ...

THIS PROJECT MATTERS TO ME BECAUSE ...

-

ONE SMALL ACTION I CAN TAKE TO MOVE FORWARD IS ...

-

OTHER THOUGHTS ...

TODAY, I'M GRATEFUL FOR ...

TODAY, I WILL STOP WORKING AT ...

_____ AM / PM

NOTES — PLAN THE DAY — BRAIN DUMP
(FREE SPACE TO HELP FREE YOUR MIND)

☀

6:00

7:00

8:00

9:00

10:00

11:00

12:00

1:00

2:00

3:00

4:00

5:00

6:00

7:00

8:00

☾

You're awesome! Go rock the day! 😊 👍 🚀 💥

TODAY I FEEL
(C'MON, BE HONEST - CIRCLE ONE)

I FEEL THIS WAY BECAUSE ...

-
-
-

TO FEEL MORE ENERGIZED I CAN ...
(WHAT PEOPLE OR ACTIVITIES GIVE YOU A BOOST?)

TODAY, MY TOP PROJECT IS ...

THIS PROJECT MATTERS TO ME BECAUSE ...

-

ONE SMALL ACTION I CAN TAKE TO MOVE FORWARD IS ...

-

OTHER THOUGHTS ...

TODAY, I'M GRATEFUL FOR ...

TODAY, I WILL STOP WORKING AT ...

_____ AM / PM

NOTES — PLAN THE DAY — BRAIN DUMP
(FREE SPACE TO HELP FREE YOUR MIND)

☀

6:00

7:00

8:00

9:00

10:00

11:00

12:00

1:00

2:00

3:00

4:00

5:00

6:00

7:00

8:00

☾

You're awesome! Go rock the day! 😉 👍 🚀 💥

TODAY I FEEL
(C'MON, BE HONEST - CIRCLE ONE)

I FEEL THIS WAY BECAUSE ...

-
-
-

TO FEEL MORE ENERGIZED I CAN ...
(WHAT PEOPLE OR ACTIVITIES GIVE YOU A BOOST?)

_____

_____

TODAY, MY TOP PROJECT IS ...

_____

_____

THIS PROJECT MATTERS TO ME BECAUSE ...

-

ONE SMALL ACTION I CAN TAKE TO MOVE FORWARD IS ...

-

OTHER THOUGHTS ...

_____

_____

_____

_____

_____

TODAY, I'M GRATEFUL FOR ...

_____

TODAY, I WILL STOP WORKING AT ...

_____ AM / PM

☀

6:00

7:00

8:00

9:00

10:00

11:00

12:00

1:00

2:00

3:00

4:00

5:00

6:00

7:00

8:00

☾

You're awesome! Go rock the day! 😉 👍 🚀 💥

TODAY I FEEL

(C'MON, BE HONEST - CIRCLE ONE)

I FEEL THIS WAY BECAUSE ...

-
-
-

TO FEEL MORE ENERGIZED I CAN ...

(WHAT PEOPLE OR ACTIVITIES GIVE YOU A BOOST?)

TODAY, MY TOP PROJECT IS ...

THIS PROJECT MATTERS TO ME BECAUSE ...

-

ONE SMALL ACTION I CAN TAKE TO MOVE FORWARD IS ...

-

OTHER THOUGHTS ...

TODAY, I'M GRATEFUL FOR ...

TODAY, I WILL STOP WORKING AT ...

_____ AM / PM

☀

6:00

7:00

8:00

9:00

10:00

11:00

12:00

1:00

2:00

3:00

4:00

5:00

6:00

7:00

8:00

☾

You're awesome! Go rock the day! 😊 👍 🚀 💥

TODAY I FEEL
(C'MON, BE HONEST - CIRCLE ONE)

I FEEL THIS WAY BECAUSE ...

-
-
-

TO FEEL MORE ENERGIZED I CAN ...
(WHAT PEOPLE OR ACTIVITIES GIVE YOU A BOOST?)

_____

_____

TODAY, MY TOP PROJECT IS ...

_____

_____

THIS PROJECT MATTERS TO ME BECAUSE ...

-

ONE SMALL ACTION I CAN TAKE TO MOVE FORWARD IS ...

-

OTHER THOUGHTS ...

_____

_____

_____

_____

_____

TODAY, I'M GRATEFUL FOR ...

_____

_____

TODAY, I WILL STOP WORKING AT ...

_____ AM / PM

☀

6:00

7:00

8:00

9:00

10:00

11:00

12:00

1:00

2:00

3:00

4:00

5:00

6:00

7:00

8:00

☾

You're awesome! Go rock the day! 😊 👍 🚀 💥

TODAY I FEEL
(C'MON, BE HONEST - CIRCLE ONE)

I FEEL THIS WAY BECAUSE ...

-
-
-

TO FEEL MORE ENERGIZED I CAN ...
(WHAT PEOPLE OR ACTIVITIES GIVE YOU A BOOST?)

_____

_____

TODAY, MY TOP PROJECT IS ...

_____

_____

THIS PROJECT MATTERS TO ME BECAUSE ...

-

ONE SMALL ACTION I CAN TAKE TO MOVE FORWARD IS ...

-

OTHER THOUGHTS ...

_____
_____
_____
_____
_____
_____

TODAY, I'M GRATEFUL FOR ...

_____
_____

TODAY, I WILL STOP WORKING AT ...

_____ AM / PM

☀

6:00

7:00

8:00

9:00

10:00

11:00

12:00

1:00

2:00

3:00

4:00

5:00

6:00

7:00

8:00

☾

You're awesome! Go rock the day! 😊 👍 🚀 💥

TODAY I FEEL
(C'MON, BE HONEST - CIRCLE ONE)

I FEEL THIS WAY BECAUSE ...

-
-
-

TO FEEL MORE ENERGIZED I CAN ...
(WHAT PEOPLE OR ACTIVITIES GIVE YOU A BOOST?)

TODAY, MY TOP PROJECT IS ...

THIS PROJECT MATTERS TO ME BECAUSE ...

-

ONE SMALL ACTION I CAN TAKE TO MOVE FORWARD IS ...

-

OTHER THOUGHTS ...

TODAY, I'M GRATEFUL FOR ...

TODAY, I WILL STOP WORKING AT ...

_____ AM / PM

NOTES — PLAN THE DAY — BRAIN DUMP
(FREE SPACE TO HELP FREE YOUR MIND)

☀

6:00

7:00

8:00

9:00

10:00

11:00

12:00

1:00

2:00

3:00

4:00

5:00

6:00

7:00

8:00

☾

You're awesome! Go rock the day! 😄 👍 🚀 💥

TODAY I FEEL
(C'MON, BE HONEST - CIRCLE ONE)

I FEEL THIS WAY BECAUSE ...

-
-
-

TO FEEL MORE ENERGIZED I CAN ...
(WHAT PEOPLE OR ACTIVITIES GIVE YOU A BOOST?)

TODAY, MY TOP PROJECT IS ...

THIS PROJECT MATTERS
TO ME BECAUSE ...

-

ONE SMALL ACTION I CAN TAKE
TO MOVE FORWARD IS ...

-

OTHER THOUGHTS ...

TODAY, I'M GRATEFUL FOR ...

TODAY, I WILL STOP WORKING AT ...

_____ AM / PM

☀

6:00

7:00

8:00

9:00

10:00

11:00

12:00

1:00

2:00

3:00

4:00

5:00

6:00

7:00

8:00

☾

You're awesome! Go rock the day! 😉 👍 🚀 💥

TODAY I FEEL
(C'MON, BE HONEST - CIRCLE ONE)

I FEEL THIS WAY BECAUSE ...

-
-
-

TO FEEL MORE ENERGIZED I CAN ...
(WHAT PEOPLE OR ACTIVITIES GIVE YOU A BOOST?)

TODAY, MY TOP PROJECT IS ...

THIS PROJECT MATTERS TO ME BECAUSE ...

-

ONE SMALL ACTION I CAN TAKE TO MOVE FORWARD IS ...

-

OTHER THOUGHTS ...

TODAY, I'M GRATEFUL FOR ...

TODAY, I WILL STOP WORKING AT ...

_____ AM / PM

NOTES — PLAN THE DAY — BRAIN DUMP

(FREE SPACE TO HELP FREE YOUR MIND)

☀

6:00

7:00

8:00

9:00

10:00

11:00

12:00

1:00

2:00

3:00

4:00

5:00

6:00

7:00

8:00

☾

You're awesome! Go rock the day! 😊 👍 🚀 💥

TODAY I FEEL
(C'MON, BE HONEST - CIRCLE ONE)

I FEEL THIS WAY BECAUSE ...

-
-
-

TO FEEL MORE ENERGIZED I CAN ...
(WHAT PEOPLE OR ACTIVITIES GIVE YOU A BOOST?)

TODAY, MY TOP PROJECT IS ...

THIS PROJECT MATTERS TO ME BECAUSE ...

-

ONE SMALL ACTION I CAN TAKE TO MOVE FORWARD IS ...

-

OTHER THOUGHTS ...

TODAY, I'M GRATEFUL FOR ...

TODAY, I WILL STOP WORKING AT ...

_____ AM / PM

NOTES — PLAN THE DAY — BRAIN DUMP
(FREE SPACE TO HELP FREE YOUR MIND)

☀

6:00

7:00

8:00

9:00

10:00

11:00

12:00

1:00

2:00

3:00

4:00

5:00

6:00

7:00

8:00

☾

You're awesome! Go rock the day! 😊 👍 🚀 💥

TIME   PLACE   DATE

TODAY I FEEL
(C'MON, BE HONEST - CIRCLE ONE)

I FEEL THIS WAY BECAUSE ...

-
-
-

TO FEEL MORE ENERGIZED I CAN ...
(WHAT PEOPLE OR ACTIVITIES GIVE YOU A BOOST?)

TODAY, MY TOP PROJECT IS ...

THIS PROJECT MATTERS TO ME BECAUSE ...

-

ONE SMALL ACTION I CAN TAKE TO MOVE FORWARD IS ...

-

OTHER THOUGHTS ...

TODAY, I'M GRATEFUL FOR ...

TODAY, I WILL STOP WORKING AT ...

_____ AM / PM

NOTES — PLAN THE DAY — BRAIN DUMP

(FREE SPACE TO HELP FREE YOUR MIND)

☀

6:00

7:00

8:00

9:00

10:00

11:00

12:00

1:00

2:00

3:00

4:00

5:00

6:00

7:00

8:00

☾

You're awesome! Go rock the day! 😊 👍 🚀 💥

TODAY I FEEL
(C'MON, BE HONEST - CIRCLE ONE)

I FEEL THIS WAY BECAUSE ...

-
-
-

TO FEEL MORE ENERGIZED I CAN ...
(WHAT PEOPLE OR ACTIVITIES GIVE YOU A BOOST?)

_____

_____

TODAY, MY TOP PROJECT IS ...

_____

_____

THIS PROJECT MATTERS TO ME BECAUSE ...

-

ONE SMALL ACTION I CAN TAKE TO MOVE FORWARD IS ...

-

OTHER THOUGHTS ...

_____

_____

_____

_____

_____

TODAY, I'M GRATEFUL FOR ...

_____

_____

TODAY, I WILL STOP WORKING AT ...

_____ AM / PM

☀

6:00

7:00

8:00

9:00

10:00

11:00

12:00

1:00

2:00

3:00

4:00

5:00

6:00

7:00

8:00

☾

You're awesome! Go rock the day! 😉 👍 🚀 💥

TODAY I FEEL
(C'MON, BE HONEST - CIRCLE ONE)

I FEEL THIS WAY BECAUSE ...

-
-
-

TO FEEL MORE ENERGIZED I CAN ...
(WHAT PEOPLE OR ACTIVITIES GIVE YOU A BOOST?)

TODAY, MY TOP PROJECT IS ...

THIS PROJECT MATTERS TO ME BECAUSE ...

-

ONE SMALL ACTION I CAN TAKE TO MOVE FORWARD IS ...

-

OTHER THOUGHTS ...

TODAY, I'M GRATEFUL FOR ...

TODAY, I WILL STOP WORKING AT ...

_____ AM / PM

☀

6:00

7:00

8:00

9:00

10:00

11:00

12:00

1:00

2:00

3:00

4:00

5:00

6:00

7:00

8:00

☾

You're awesome! Go rock the day! 😊 👍 🚀 💥

TODAY I FEEL
(C'MON, BE HONEST - CIRCLE ONE)

I FEEL THIS WAY BECAUSE ...

-
-
-

TO FEEL MORE ENERGIZED I CAN ...
(WHAT PEOPLE OR ACTIVITIES GIVE YOU A BOOST?)

_____

_____

TODAY, MY TOP PROJECT IS ...

_____

_____

THIS PROJECT MATTERS TO ME BECAUSE ...

-

ONE SMALL ACTION I CAN TAKE TO MOVE FORWARD IS ...

-

OTHER THOUGHTS ...

_____

_____

_____

_____

_____

TODAY, I'M GRATEFUL FOR ...

_____

_____

TODAY, I WILL STOP WORKING AT ...

_____ AM / PM

NOTES — PLAN THE DAY — BRAIN DUMP
(FREE SPACE TO HELP FREE YOUR MIND)

☀

6:00

7:00

8:00

9:00

10:00

11:00

12:00

1:00

2:00

3:00

4:00

5:00

6:00

7:00

8:00

☾

You're awesome! Go rock the day! 😉 👍 🚀 💥

TODAY I FEEL
(C'MON, BE HONEST - CIRCLE ONE)

I FEEL THIS WAY BECAUSE ...

-
-
-

TO FEEL MORE ENERGIZED I CAN ...
(WHAT PEOPLE OR ACTIVITIES GIVE YOU A BOOST?)

_____

_____

TODAY, MY TOP PROJECT IS ...

_____

_____

THIS PROJECT MATTERS TO ME BECAUSE ...

-

ONE SMALL ACTION I CAN TAKE TO MOVE FORWARD IS ...

-

OTHER THOUGHTS ...

_____

_____

_____

_____

_____

_____

TODAY, I'M GRATEFUL FOR ...

_____

_____

TODAY, I WILL STOP WORKING AT ...

_____ AM / PM

☀

6:00

7:00

8:00

9:00

10:00

11:00

12:00

1:00

2:00

3:00

4:00

5:00

6:00

7:00

8:00

☾

You're awesome! Go rock the day!

TODAY I FEEL
(C'MON, BE HONEST - CIRCLE ONE)

I FEEL THIS WAY BECAUSE ...

-
-
-

TO FEEL MORE ENERGIZED I CAN ...
(WHAT PEOPLE OR ACTIVITIES GIVE YOU A BOOST?)

TODAY, MY TOP PROJECT IS ...

THIS PROJECT MATTERS TO ME BECAUSE ...

-

ONE SMALL ACTION I CAN TAKE TO MOVE FORWARD IS ...

-

OTHER THOUGHTS ...

TODAY, I'M GRATEFUL FOR ...

TODAY, I WILL STOP WORKING AT ...

_____ AM / PM

NOTES — PLAN THE DAY — BRAIN DUMP
(FREE SPACE TO HELP FREE YOUR MIND)

☀

6:00

7:00

8:00

9:00

10:00

11:00

12:00

1:00

2:00

3:00

4:00

5:00

6:00

7:00

8:00

☾

You're awesome! Go rock the day! 😊 👍 🚀 💥

TODAY I FEEL
(C'MON, BE HONEST - CIRCLE ONE)

I FEEL THIS WAY BECAUSE ...

-
-
-

TO FEEL MORE ENERGIZED I CAN ...
(WHAT PEOPLE OR ACTIVITIES GIVE YOU A BOOST?)

TODAY, MY TOP PROJECT IS ...

THIS PROJECT MATTERS TO ME BECAUSE ...

-

OTHER THOUGHTS ...

ONE SMALL ACTION I CAN TAKE TO MOVE FORWARD IS ...

-

TODAY, I'M GRATEFUL FOR ...

TODAY, I WILL STOP WORKING AT ...

_____ AM / PM

☀️

6:00

7:00

8:00

9:00

10:00

11:00

12:00

1:00

2:00

3:00

4:00

5:00

6:00

7:00

8:00

☾

You're awesome! Go rock the day! 😊 👍 🚀 💥

TODAY I FEEL
(C'MON, BE HONEST - CIRCLE ONE)

I FEEL THIS WAY BECAUSE ...

-
-
-

TO FEEL MORE ENERGIZED I CAN ...
(WHAT PEOPLE OR ACTIVITIES GIVE YOU A BOOST?)

TODAY, MY TOP PROJECT IS ...

THIS PROJECT MATTERS TO ME BECAUSE ...

-

ONE SMALL ACTION I CAN TAKE TO MOVE FORWARD IS ...

-

OTHER THOUGHTS ...

TODAY, I'M GRATEFUL FOR ...

TODAY, I WILL STOP WORKING AT ...

_____ AM / PM

6:00

7:00

8:00

9:00

10:00

11:00

12:00

1:00

2:00

3:00

4:00

5:00

6:00

7:00

8:00

You're awesome! Go rock the day!

TIME   PLACE   DATE

TODAY I FEEL
(C'MON, BE HONEST - CIRCLE ONE)

I FEEL THIS WAY BECAUSE ...

-
-
-

TO FEEL MORE ENERGIZED I CAN ...
(WHAT PEOPLE OR ACTIVITIES GIVE YOU A BOOST?)

TODAY, MY TOP PROJECT IS ...

THIS PROJECT MATTERS TO ME BECAUSE ...

-

ONE SMALL ACTION I CAN TAKE TO MOVE FORWARD IS ...

-

OTHER THOUGHTS ...

TODAY, I'M GRATEFUL FOR ...

TODAY, I WILL STOP WORKING AT ...

_____ AM / PM

NOTES — PLAN THE DAY — BRAIN DUMP

(FREE SPACE TO HELP FREE YOUR MIND)

☀

6:00

7:00

8:00

9:00

10:00

11:00

12:00

1:00

2:00

3:00

4:00

5:00

6:00

7:00

8:00

☾

You're awesome! Go rock the day! 😊 👍 🚀 💥

TIME   ● PLACE   DATE

TODAY I FEEL
(C'MON, BE HONEST - CIRCLE ONE)

I FEEL THIS WAY BECAUSE ...

-
-
-

TO FEEL MORE ENERGIZED I CAN ...
(WHAT PEOPLE OR ACTIVITIES GIVE YOU A BOOST?)

TODAY, MY TOP PROJECT IS ...

THIS PROJECT MATTERS TO ME BECAUSE ...

-

ONE SMALL ACTION I CAN TAKE TO MOVE FORWARD IS ...

-

OTHER THOUGHTS ...

TODAY, I'M GRATEFUL FOR ...

TODAY, I WILL STOP WORKING AT ...

_____ AM / PM

NOTES — PLAN THE DAY — BRAIN DUMP
(FREE SPACE TO HELP FREE YOUR MIND)

☀

6:00

7:00

8:00

9:00

10:00

11:00

12:00

1:00

2:00

3:00

4:00

5:00

6:00

7:00

8:00

☾

You're awesome! Go rock the day! 😊 👍 🚀 💥

TODAY I FEEL
(C'MON, BE HONEST - CIRCLE ONE)

I FEEL THIS WAY BECAUSE ...

-
-
-

TO FEEL MORE ENERGIZED I CAN ...
(WHAT PEOPLE OR ACTIVITIES GIVE YOU A BOOST?)

_____

_____

TODAY, MY TOP PROJECT IS ...

_____

_____

THIS PROJECT MATTERS TO ME BECAUSE ...

-

ONE SMALL ACTION I CAN TAKE TO MOVE FORWARD IS ...

-

OTHER THOUGHTS ...

_____
_____
_____
_____
_____

TODAY, I'M GRATEFUL FOR ...

_____
_____

TODAY, I WILL STOP WORKING AT ...

_____ AM / PM

☀

6:00

7:00

8:00

9:00

10:00

11:00

12:00

1:00

2:00

3:00

4:00

5:00

6:00

7:00

8:00

☾

You're awesome! Go rock the day! 😊 👍 🚀 💥

TODAY I FEEL
(C'MON, BE HONEST - CIRCLE ONE)

I FEEL THIS WAY BECAUSE ...

-
-
-

TO FEEL MORE ENERGIZED I CAN ...
(WHAT PEOPLE OR ACTIVITIES GIVE YOU A BOOST?)

_____

_____

TODAY, MY TOP PROJECT IS ...

_____

_____

THIS PROJECT MATTERS TO ME BECAUSE ...

-

ONE SMALL ACTION I CAN TAKE TO MOVE FORWARD IS ...

-

OTHER THOUGHTS ...

_____
_____
_____
_____
_____
_____

TODAY, I'M GRATEFUL FOR ...

_____
_____

TODAY, I WILL STOP WORKING AT ...

_____ AM / PM

NOTES — PLAN THE DAY — BRAIN DUMP
(FREE SPACE TO HELP FREE YOUR MIND)

☀

6:00

7:00

8:00

9:00

10:00

11:00

12:00

1:00

2:00

3:00

4:00

5:00

6:00

7:00

8:00

☾

You're awesome! Go rock the day! 😊 👍 🚀 💥

TODAY I FEEL
(C'MON, BE HONEST - CIRCLE ONE)

I FEEL THIS WAY BECAUSE ...

-
-
-

TO FEEL MORE ENERGIZED I CAN ...
(WHAT PEOPLE OR ACTIVITIES GIVE YOU A BOOST?)

_____

_____

TODAY, MY TOP PROJECT IS ...

_____

_____

THIS PROJECT MATTERS TO ME BECAUSE ...

-

ONE SMALL ACTION I CAN TAKE TO MOVE FORWARD IS ...

-

OTHER THOUGHTS ...

_____

_____

_____

_____

_____

TODAY, I'M GRATEFUL FOR ...

_____

TODAY, I WILL STOP WORKING AT ...

_____ AM / PM

☀

6:00

7:00

8:00

9:00

10:00

11:00

12:00

1:00

2:00

3:00

4:00

5:00

6:00

7:00

8:00

☾

You're awesome! Go rock the day! 😊👍🚀💥

TODAY I FEEL
(C'MON, BE HONEST - CIRCLE ONE)

I FEEL THIS WAY BECAUSE ...

-
-
-

TO FEEL MORE ENERGIZED I CAN ...
(WHAT PEOPLE OR ACTIVITIES GIVE YOU A BOOST?)

TODAY, MY TOP PROJECT IS ...

THIS PROJECT MATTERS TO ME BECAUSE ...

-

ONE SMALL ACTION I CAN TAKE TO MOVE FORWARD IS ...

-

OTHER THOUGHTS ...

TODAY, I'M GRATEFUL FOR ...

TODAY, I WILL STOP WORKING AT ...

_____ AM / PM

NOTES — PLAN THE DAY — BRAIN DUMP
(FREE SPACE TO HELP FREE YOUR MIND)

☀

6:00

7:00

8:00

9:00

10:00

11:00

12:00

1:00

2:00

3:00

4:00

5:00

6:00

7:00

8:00

☾

You're awesome! Go rock the day! 😌 👍 🚀 💥

TODAY I FEEL
(C'MON, BE HONEST - CIRCLE ONE)

I FEEL THIS WAY BECAUSE ...

-
-
-

TO FEEL MORE ENERGIZED I CAN ...
(WHAT PEOPLE OR ACTIVITIES GIVE YOU A BOOST?)

TODAY, MY TOP PROJECT IS ...

THIS PROJECT MATTERS TO ME BECAUSE ...

-

ONE SMALL ACTION I CAN TAKE TO MOVE FORWARD IS ...

-

OTHER THOUGHTS ...

TODAY, I'M GRATEFUL FOR ...

TODAY, I WILL STOP WORKING AT ...

_____ AM / PM

NOTES — PLAN THE DAY — BRAIN DUMP
(FREE SPACE TO HELP FREE YOUR MIND)

☀

6:00

7:00

8:00

9:00

10:00

11:00

12:00

1:00

2:00

3:00

4:00

5:00

6:00

7:00

8:00

☾

You're awesome! Go rock the day! 😊 👍 🚀 💥

TODAY I FEEL
(C'MON, BE HONEST - CIRCLE ONE)

I FEEL THIS WAY BECAUSE ...

-
-
-

TO FEEL MORE ENERGIZED I CAN ...
(WHAT PEOPLE OR ACTIVITIES GIVE YOU A BOOST?)

TODAY, MY TOP PROJECT IS ...

THIS PROJECT MATTERS TO ME BECAUSE ...

-

ONE SMALL ACTION I CAN TAKE TO MOVE FORWARD IS ...

-

OTHER THOUGHTS ...

TODAY, I'M GRATEFUL FOR ...

TODAY, I WILL STOP WORKING AT ...

_____ AM / PM

6:00

7:00

8:00

9:00

10:00

11:00

12:00

1:00

2:00

3:00

4:00

5:00

6:00

7:00

8:00

You're awesome! Go rock the day!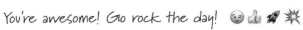

TODAY I FEEL

(C'MON, BE HONEST - CIRCLE ONE)

I FEEL THIS WAY BECAUSE ...

-
-
-

TO FEEL MORE ENERGIZED I CAN ...
(WHAT PEOPLE OR ACTIVITIES GIVE YOU A BOOST?)

TODAY, MY TOP PROJECT IS ...

THIS PROJECT MATTERS TO ME BECAUSE ...

-

ONE SMALL ACTION I CAN TAKE TO MOVE FORWARD IS ...

-

OTHER THOUGHTS ...

TODAY, I'M GRATEFUL FOR ...

TODAY, I WILL STOP WORKING AT ...

_____ AM / PM

☀

6:00

7:00

8:00

9:00

10:00

11:00

12:00

1:00

2:00

3:00

4:00

5:00

6:00

7:00

8:00

☾

You're awesome! Go rock the day! 😊 👍 🚀 💥

TODAY I FEEL
(C'MON, BE HONEST - CIRCLE ONE)

I FEEL THIS WAY BECAUSE ...

-
-
-

TO FEEL MORE ENERGIZED I CAN ...
(WHAT PEOPLE OR ACTIVITIES GIVE YOU A BOOST?)

TODAY, MY TOP PROJECT IS ...

THIS PROJECT MATTERS TO ME BECAUSE ...

-

ONE SMALL ACTION I CAN TAKE TO MOVE FORWARD IS ...

-

OTHER THOUGHTS ...

TODAY, I'M GRATEFUL FOR ...

TODAY, I WILL STOP WORKING AT ...

_____ AM / PM

☀

6:00

7:00

8:00

9:00

10:00

11:00

12:00

1:00

2:00

3:00

4:00

5:00

6:00

7:00

8:00

☾

You're awesome! Go rock the day! 😊 👍 🚀 💥

TODAY I FEEL
(C'MON, BE HONEST - CIRCLE ONE)

I FEEL THIS WAY BECAUSE ...

-
-
-

TO FEEL MORE ENERGIZED I CAN ...
(WHAT PEOPLE OR ACTIVITIES GIVE YOU A BOOST?)

TODAY, MY TOP PROJECT IS ...

THIS PROJECT MATTERS TO ME BECAUSE ...

-

ONE SMALL ACTION I CAN TAKE TO MOVE FORWARD IS ...

-

OTHER THOUGHTS ...

TODAY, I'M GRATEFUL FOR ....

TODAY, I WILL STOP WORKING AT ...

_____ AM / PM

NOTES — PLAN THE DAY — BRAIN DUMP
(FREE SPACE TO HELP FREE YOUR MIND)

☀

6:00

7:00

8:00

9:00

10:00

11:00

12:00

1:00

2:00

3:00

4:00

5:00

6:00

7:00

8:00

☾

You're awesome! Go rock the day! 😉 👍 🚀 💥

TODAY I FEEL
(C'MON, BE HONEST - CIRCLE ONE)

I FEEL THIS WAY BECAUSE ...

-
-
-

TO FEEL MORE ENERGIZED I CAN ...
(WHAT PEOPLE OR ACTIVITIES GIVE YOU A BOOST?)

_____

_____

TODAY, MY TOP PROJECT IS ...

_____

_____

THIS PROJECT MATTERS TO ME BECAUSE ...

-

ONE SMALL ACTION I CAN TAKE TO MOVE FORWARD IS ...

-

OTHER THOUGHTS ...

_____
_____
_____
_____
_____
_____

TODAY, I'M GRATEFUL FOR ...

_____

TODAY, I WILL STOP WORKING AT ...

_____ AM / PM

☀

6:00

7:00

8:00

9:00

10:00

11:00

12:00

1:00

2:00

3:00

4:00

5:00

6:00

7:00

8:00

☾

You're awesome! Go rock the day! 😊 👍 🚀 💥

TODAY I FEEL
(C'MON, BE HONEST - CIRCLE ONE)

I FEEL THIS WAY BECAUSE ...

-
-
-

TO FEEL MORE ENERGIZED I CAN ...
(WHAT PEOPLE OR ACTIVITIES GIVE YOU A BOOST?)

TODAY, MY TOP PROJECT IS ...

THIS PROJECT MATTERS TO ME BECAUSE ...

-

ONE SMALL ACTION I CAN TAKE TO MOVE FORWARD IS ...

-

OTHER THOUGHTS ...

TODAY, I'M GRATEFUL FOR ...

TODAY, I WILL STOP WORKING AT ...

_____ AM / PM

NOTES — PLAN THE DAY — BRAIN DUMP
(FREE SPACE TO HELP FREE YOUR MIND)

☀

6:00

7:00

8:00

9:00

10:00

11:00

12:00

1:00

2:00

3:00

4:00

5:00

6:00

7:00

8:00

☾

You're awesome! Go rock the day! 😉 👍 🚀 💥

TODAY I FEEL
(C'MON, BE HONEST - CIRCLE ONE)

I FEEL THIS WAY BECAUSE ...

-
-
-

TO FEEL MORE ENERGIZED I CAN ...
(WHAT PEOPLE OR ACTIVITIES GIVE YOU A BOOST?)

TODAY, MY TOP PROJECT IS ...

THIS PROJECT MATTERS TO ME BECAUSE ...

-

ONE SMALL ACTION I CAN TAKE TO MOVE FORWARD IS ...

-

OTHER THOUGHTS ...

TODAY, I'M GRATEFUL FOR ...

TODAY, I WILL STOP WORKING AT ...

_____ AM / PM

NOTES — PLAN THE DAY — BRAIN DUMP
(FREE SPACE TO HELP FREE YOUR MIND)

☀️

6:00

7:00

8:00

9:00

10:00

11:00

12:00

1:00

2:00

3:00

4:00

5:00

6:00

7:00

8:00

🌙

You're awesome! Go rock the day! 😊 👍 🚀 💥

TODAY I FEEL
(C'MON, BE HONEST - CIRCLE ONE)

I FEEL THIS WAY BECAUSE ...

-
-
-

TO FEEL MORE ENERGIZED I CAN ...
(WHAT PEOPLE OR ACTIVITIES GIVE YOU A BOOST?)

TODAY, MY TOP PROJECT IS ...

THIS PROJECT MATTERS TO ME BECAUSE ...

-

ONE SMALL ACTION I CAN TAKE TO MOVE FORWARD IS ...

-

OTHER THOUGHTS ...

TODAY, I'M GRATEFUL FOR ...

TODAY, I WILL STOP WORKING AT ...

_____ AM / PM

☀

6:00

7:00

8:00

9:00

10:00

11:00

12:00

1:00

2:00

3:00

4:00

5:00

6:00

7:00

8:00

☾

You're awesome! Go rock the day! 😉 👍 🚀 💥

TODAY I FEEL
(C'MON, BE HONEST - CIRCLE ONE)

I FEEL THIS WAY BECAUSE ...

-
-
-

TO FEEL MORE ENERGIZED I CAN ...
(WHAT PEOPLE OR ACTIVITIES GIVE YOU A BOOST?)

TODAY, MY TOP PROJECT IS ...

THIS PROJECT MATTERS TO ME BECAUSE ...

-

ONE SMALL ACTION I CAN TAKE TO MOVE FORWARD IS ...

-

OTHER THOUGHTS ...

TODAY, I'M GRATEFUL FOR ...

TODAY, I WILL STOP WORKING AT ...

_____ AM / PM

☀

6:00

7:00

8:00

9:00

10:00

11:00

12:00

1:00

2:00

3:00

4:00

5:00

6:00

7:00

8:00

☾

You're awesome! Go rock the day! 😊 👍 🚀 💥

TODAY I FEEL

(C'MON, BE HONEST - CIRCLE ONE)

I FEEL THIS WAY BECAUSE ...

-
-
-

TO FEEL MORE ENERGIZED I CAN ...

(WHAT PEOPLE OR ACTIVITIES GIVE YOU A BOOST?)

TODAY, MY TOP PROJECT IS ...

THIS PROJECT MATTERS TO ME BECAUSE ...

-

ONE SMALL ACTION I CAN TAKE TO MOVE FORWARD IS ...

-

OTHER THOUGHTS ...

TODAY, I'M GRATEFUL FOR ...

TODAY, I WILL STOP WORKING AT ...

_____ AM / PM

NOTES — PLAN THE DAY — BRAIN DUMP
(FREE SPACE TO HELP FREE YOUR MIND)

☀

6:00

7:00

8:00

9:00

10:00

11:00

12:00

1:00

2:00

3:00

4:00

5:00

6:00

7:00

8:00

☾

You're awesome! Go rock the day! 😊 👍 🚀 💥

TODAY I FEEL
(C'MON, BE HONEST - CIRCLE ONE)

I FEEL THIS WAY BECAUSE ...

-
-
-

TO FEEL MORE ENERGIZED I CAN ...
(WHAT PEOPLE OR ACTIVITIES GIVE YOU A BOOST?)

TODAY, MY TOP PROJECT IS ...

THIS PROJECT MATTERS TO ME BECAUSE ...

-

ONE SMALL ACTION I CAN TAKE TO MOVE FORWARD IS ...

-

OTHER THOUGHTS ...

TODAY, I'M GRATEFUL FOR ...

TODAY, I WILL STOP WORKING AT ...

_____ AM / PM

NOTES — PLAN THE DAY — BRAIN DUMP
(FREE SPACE TO HELP FREE YOUR MIND)

☀

6:00

7:00

8:00

9:00

10:00

11:00

12:00

1:00

2:00

3:00

4:00

5:00

6:00

7:00

8:00

☾

You're awesome! Go rock the day! 😊 👍 🚀 💥

TODAY I FEEL
(C'MON, BE HONEST - CIRCLE ONE)

I FEEL THIS WAY BECAUSE ...

-
-
-

TO FEEL MORE ENERGIZED I CAN ...
(WHAT PEOPLE OR ACTIVITIES GIVE YOU A BOOST?)

TODAY, MY TOP PROJECT IS ...

THIS PROJECT MATTERS TO ME BECAUSE ...

-

ONE SMALL ACTION I CAN TAKE TO MOVE FORWARD IS ...

-

OTHER THOUGHTS ...

TODAY, I'M GRATEFUL FOR ...

TODAY, I WILL STOP WORKING AT ...

_____ AM / PM

NOTES — PLAN THE DAY — BRAIN DUMP
(FREE SPACE TO HELP FREE YOUR MIND)

☀

6:00

7:00

8:00

9:00

10:00

11:00

12:00

1:00

2:00

3:00

4:00

5:00

6:00

7:00

8:00

☾

You're awesome! Go rock the day! 😊 👍 🚀 💥

TODAY I FEEL
(C'MON, BE HONEST - CIRCLE ONE)

I FEEL THIS WAY BECAUSE ...

-
-
-

TO FEEL MORE ENERGIZED I CAN ...
(WHAT PEOPLE OR ACTIVITIES GIVE YOU A BOOST?)

TODAY, MY TOP PROJECT IS ...

THIS PROJECT MATTERS TO ME BECAUSE ...

-

ONE SMALL ACTION I CAN TAKE TO MOVE FORWARD IS ...

-

OTHER THOUGHTS ...

TODAY, I'M GRATEFUL FOR ...

TODAY, I WILL STOP WORKING AT ...

_____ AM / PM

☀

6:00

7:00

8:00

9:00

10:00

11:00

12:00

1:00

2:00

3:00

4:00

5:00

6:00

7:00

8:00

☾

You're awesome! Go rock the day! 😉 👍 🚀 💥

TODAY I FEEL
(C'MON, BE HONEST - CIRCLE ONE)

I FEEL THIS WAY BECAUSE ...

-
-
-

TO FEEL MORE ENERGIZED I CAN ...
(WHAT PEOPLE OR ACTIVITIES GIVE YOU A BOOST?)

TODAY, MY TOP PROJECT IS ...

THIS PROJECT MATTERS TO ME BECAUSE ...

-

ONE SMALL ACTION I CAN TAKE TO MOVE FORWARD IS ...

-

OTHER THOUGHTS ...

TODAY, I'M GRATEFUL FOR ...

TODAY, I WILL STOP WORKING AT ...

_____ AM / PM

NOTES — PLAN THE DAY — BRAIN DUMP

(FREE SPACE TO HELP FREE YOUR MIND)

☀

6:00

7:00

8:00

9:00

10:00

11:00

12:00

1:00

2:00

3:00

4:00

5:00

6:00

7:00

8:00

☾

You're awesome! Go rock the day! 😉 👍 🚀 💥

TIME   PLACE   DATE

TODAY I FEEL
(C'MON, BE HONEST - CIRCLE ONE)

I FEEL THIS WAY BECAUSE ...

-
-
-

TO FEEL MORE ENERGIZED I CAN ...
(WHAT PEOPLE OR ACTIVITIES GIVE YOU A BOOST?)

TODAY, MY TOP PROJECT IS ...

THIS PROJECT MATTERS TO ME BECAUSE ...

-

ONE SMALL ACTION I CAN TAKE TO MOVE FORWARD IS ...

-

OTHER THOUGHTS ...

TODAY, I'M GRATEFUL FOR ...

TODAY, I WILL STOP WORKING AT ...

_____ AM / PM

☀

6:00

7:00

8:00

9:00

10:00

11:00

12:00

1:00

2:00

3:00

4:00

5:00

6:00

7:00

8:00

☾

You're awesome! Go rock the day! 😉 👍 🚀 💥

TODAY I FEEL
(C'MON, BE HONEST - CIRCLE ONE)

I FEEL THIS WAY BECAUSE ...

-
-
-

TO FEEL MORE ENERGIZED I CAN ...
(WHAT PEOPLE OR ACTIVITIES GIVE YOU A BOOST?)

TODAY, MY TOP PROJECT IS ...

THIS PROJECT MATTERS TO ME BECAUSE ...

-

ONE SMALL ACTION I CAN TAKE TO MOVE FORWARD IS ...

-

OTHER THOUGHTS ...

TODAY, I'M GRATEFUL FOR ...

TODAY, I WILL STOP WORKING AT ...

_____ AM / PM

☀

6:00

7:00

8:00

9:00

10:00

11:00

12:00

1:00

2:00

3:00

4:00

5:00

6:00

7:00

8:00

☾

You're awesome! Go rock the day! 😊 👍 🚀 💥

TIME   📍 PLACE   DATE

TODAY I FEEL
(C'MON, BE HONEST - CIRCLE ONE)

I FEEL THIS WAY BECAUSE ...

-
-
-

TO FEEL MORE ENERGIZED I CAN ...
(WHAT PEOPLE OR ACTIVITIES GIVE YOU A BOOST?)

_____

_____

TODAY, MY TOP PROJECT IS ...

_____

_____

THIS PROJECT MATTERS TO ME BECAUSE ...

-

ONE SMALL ACTION I CAN TAKE TO MOVE FORWARD IS ...

-

OTHER THOUGHTS ...

_____
_____
_____
_____
_____
_____

TODAY, I'M GRATEFUL FOR ...

_____

TODAY, I WILL STOP WORKING AT ...

_____ AM / PM

NOTES — PLAN THE DAY — BRAIN DUMP

(FREE SPACE TO HELP FREE YOUR MIND)

☀

6:00

7:00

8:00

9:00

10:00

11:00

12:00

1:00

2:00

3:00

4:00

5:00

6:00

7:00

8:00

☾

You're awesome! Go rock the day! 😊 👍 🚀 💥

TODAY I FEEL
(C'MON, BE HONEST - CIRCLE ONE)

I FEEL THIS WAY BECAUSE ...

-
-
-

TO FEEL MORE ENERGIZED I CAN ...
(WHAT PEOPLE OR ACTIVITIES GIVE YOU A BOOST?)

TODAY, MY TOP PROJECT IS ...

THIS PROJECT MATTERS TO ME BECAUSE ...

-

ONE SMALL ACTION I CAN TAKE TO MOVE FORWARD IS ...

-

OTHER THOUGHTS ...

TODAY, I'M GRATEFUL FOR ...

TODAY, I WILL STOP WORKING AT ...

_____ AM / PM

NOTES — PLAN THE DAY — BRAIN DUMP
(FREE SPACE TO HELP FREE YOUR MIND)

☀

6:00

7:00

8:00

9:00

10:00

11:00

12:00

1:00

2:00

3:00

4:00

5:00

6:00

7:00

8:00

☾

You're awesome! Go rock the day! 😊 👍 🚀 💥

TODAY I FEEL
(C'MON, BE HONEST - CIRCLE ONE)

I FEEL THIS WAY BECAUSE ...

-
-
-

TO FEEL MORE ENERGIZED I CAN ...
(WHAT PEOPLE OR ACTIVITIES GIVE YOU A BOOST?)

TODAY, MY TOP PROJECT IS ...

THIS PROJECT MATTERS TO ME BECAUSE ...

-

ONE SMALL ACTION I CAN TAKE TO MOVE FORWARD IS ...

-

OTHER THOUGHTS ...

TODAY, I'M GRATEFUL FOR ...

TODAY, I WILL STOP WORKING AT ...

_____ AM / PM

☀️

6:00

7:00

8:00

9:00

10:00

11:00

12:00

1:00

2:00

3:00

4:00

5:00

6:00

7:00

8:00

🌙

You're awesome! Go rock the day! 😉 👍 🚀 💥

TODAY I FEEL
(C'MON, BE HONEST - CIRCLE ONE)

I FEEL THIS WAY BECAUSE ...

-
-
-

TO FEEL MORE ENERGIZED I CAN ...
(WHAT PEOPLE OR ACTIVITIES GIVE YOU A BOOST?)

TODAY, MY TOP PROJECT IS ...

THIS PROJECT MATTERS TO ME BECAUSE ...

-

ONE SMALL ACTION I CAN TAKE TO MOVE FORWARD IS ...

-

OTHER THOUGHTS ...

TODAY, I'M GRATEFUL FOR ...

TODAY, I WILL STOP WORKING AT ...

_____ AM / PM

☀

6:00

7:00

8:00

9:00

10:00

11:00

12:00

1:00

2:00

3:00

4:00

5:00

6:00

7:00

8:00

☾

You're awesome! Go rock the day! 😄 👍 🚀 💥

TODAY I FEEL
(C'MON, BE HONEST - CIRCLE ONE)

I FEEL THIS WAY BECAUSE ...

-
-
-

TO FEEL MORE ENERGIZED I CAN ...
(WHAT PEOPLE OR ACTIVITIES GIVE YOU A BOOST?)

TODAY, MY TOP PROJECT IS ...

THIS PROJECT MATTERS TO ME BECAUSE ...

-

ONE SMALL ACTION I CAN TAKE TO MOVE FORWARD IS ...

-

OTHER THOUGHTS ...

TODAY, I'M GRATEFUL FOR ...

TODAY, I WILL STOP WORKING AT ...

_____ AM / PM

☀

6:00

7:00

8:00

9:00

10:00

11:00

12:00

1:00

2:00

3:00

4:00

5:00

6:00

7:00

8:00

☾

You're awesome! Go rock the day! 😉 👍 🚀 💥

TODAY I FEEL
(C'MON, BE HONEST - CIRCLE ONE)

I FEEL THIS WAY BECAUSE ...

-
-
-

TO FEEL MORE ENERGIZED I CAN ...
(WHAT PEOPLE OR ACTIVITIES GIVE YOU A BOOST?)

TODAY, MY TOP PROJECT IS ...

THIS PROJECT MATTERS TO ME BECAUSE ...

-

ONE SMALL ACTION I CAN TAKE TO MOVE FORWARD IS ...

-

OTHER THOUGHTS ...

TODAY, I'M GRATEFUL FOR ...

TODAY, I WILL STOP WORKING AT ...

_____ AM / PM

NOTES — PLAN THE DAY — BRAIN DUMP
(FREE SPACE TO HELP FREE YOUR MIND)

☀

6:00

7:00

8:00

9:00

10:00

11:00

12:00

1:00

2:00

3:00

4:00

5:00

6:00

7:00

8:00

☾

You're awesome! Go rock the day! 😊 👍 🚀 💥

TODAY I FEEL
(C'MON, BE HONEST - CIRCLE ONE)

I FEEL THIS WAY BECAUSE ...

- •
- •
- •

TO FEEL MORE ENERGIZED I CAN ...
(WHAT PEOPLE OR ACTIVITIES GIVE YOU A BOOST?)

TODAY, MY TOP PROJECT IS ...

THIS PROJECT MATTERS TO ME BECAUSE ...

- •

ONE SMALL ACTION I CAN TAKE TO MOVE FORWARD IS ...

- •

OTHER THOUGHTS ...

TODAY, I'M GRATEFUL FOR ...

TODAY, I WILL STOP WORKING AT ...

_____ AM / PM

☀

6:00

7:00

8:00

9:00

10:00

11:00

12:00

1:00

2:00

3:00

4:00

5:00

6:00

7:00

8:00

☾

You're awesome! Go rock the day! 😊 👍 🚀 💥

TODAY I FEEL
(C'MON, BE HONEST - CIRCLE ONE)

I FEEL THIS WAY BECAUSE ...

-
-
-

TO FEEL MORE ENERGIZED I CAN ...
(WHAT PEOPLE OR ACTIVITIES GIVE YOU A BOOST?)

TODAY, MY TOP PROJECT IS ...

THIS PROJECT MATTERS TO ME BECAUSE ...

-

ONE SMALL ACTION I CAN TAKE TO MOVE FORWARD IS ...

-

OTHER THOUGHTS ...

TODAY, I'M GRATEFUL FOR ...

TODAY, I WILL STOP WORKING AT ...

_____ AM / PM

NOTES — PLAN THE DAY — BRAIN DUMP
(FREE SPACE TO HELP FREE YOUR MIND)

☀

6:00

7:00

8:00

9:00

10:00

11:00

12:00

1:00

2:00

3:00

4:00

5:00

6:00

7:00

8:00

☾

You're awesome! Go rock the day! 😊 👍 🚀 💥

TODAY I FEEL
(C'MON, BE HONEST - CIRCLE ONE)

I FEEL THIS WAY BECAUSE ...

-
-
-

TO FEEL MORE ENERGIZED I CAN ...
(WHAT PEOPLE OR ACTIVITIES GIVE YOU A BOOST?)

TODAY, MY TOP PROJECT IS ...

THIS PROJECT MATTERS TO ME BECAUSE ...

-

ONE SMALL ACTION I CAN TAKE TO MOVE FORWARD IS ...

-

OTHER THOUGHTS ...

TODAY, I'M GRATEFUL FOR ...

TODAY, I WILL STOP WORKING AT ...

_____ AM / PM

NOTES — PLAN THE DAY — BRAIN DUMP
(FREE SPACE TO HELP FREE YOUR MIND)

☀

6:00

7:00

8:00

9:00

10:00

11:00

12:00

1:00

2:00

3:00

4:00

5:00

6:00

7:00

8:00

☾

You're awesome! Go rock the day! 😊 👍 🚀 💥

TODAY I FEEL
(C'MON, BE HONEST - CIRCLE ONE)

I FEEL THIS WAY BECAUSE ...

-
-
-

TO FEEL MORE ENERGIZED I CAN ...
(WHAT PEOPLE OR ACTIVITIES GIVE YOU A BOOST?)

TODAY, MY TOP PROJECT IS ...

THIS PROJECT MATTERS TO ME BECAUSE ...

-

ONE SMALL ACTION I CAN TAKE TO MOVE FORWARD IS ...

-

OTHER THOUGHTS ...

TODAY, I'M GRATEFUL FOR ...

TODAY, I WILL STOP WORKING AT ...

_____ AM / PM

☀

6:00

7:00

8:00

9:00

10:00

11:00

12:00

1:00

2:00

3:00

4:00

5:00

6:00

7:00

8:00

☾

You're awesome! Go rock the day! 😌 👍 🚀 💥

TODAY I FEEL
(C'MON, BE HONEST - CIRCLE ONE)

I FEEL THIS WAY BECAUSE ...

-
-
-

TO FEEL MORE ENERGIZED I CAN ...
(WHAT PEOPLE OR ACTIVITIES GIVE YOU A BOOST?)

TODAY, MY TOP PROJECT IS ...

THIS PROJECT MATTERS TO ME BECAUSE ...

-

ONE SMALL ACTION I CAN TAKE TO MOVE FORWARD IS ...

-

OTHER THOUGHTS ...

TODAY, I'M GRATEFUL FOR ...

TODAY, I WILL STOP WORKING AT ...

_____ AM / PM

NOTES — PLAN THE DAY — BRAIN DUMP

(FREE SPACE TO HELP FREE YOUR MIND)

☀

6:00

7:00

8:00

9:00

10:00

11:00

12:00

1:00

2:00

3:00

4:00

5:00

6:00

7:00

8:00

☾

You're awesome! Go rock the day! 😜 👍 🚀 💥

TODAY I FEEL
(C'MON, BE HONEST - CIRCLE ONE)

I FEEL THIS WAY BECAUSE ...

-
-
-

TO FEEL MORE ENERGIZED I CAN ...
(WHAT PEOPLE OR ACTIVITIES GIVE YOU A BOOST?)

TODAY, MY TOP PROJECT IS ...

THIS PROJECT MATTERS TO ME BECAUSE ...

-

ONE SMALL ACTION I CAN TAKE TO MOVE FORWARD IS ...

-

OTHER THOUGHTS ...

TODAY, I'M GRATEFUL FOR ...

TODAY, I WILL STOP WORKING AT ...

_____ AM / PM

☀

6:00

7:00

8:00

9:00

10:00

11:00

12:00

1:00

2:00

3:00

4:00

5:00

6:00

7:00

8:00

☾

You're awesome! Go rock the day! 😊 👍 🚀 💥

TODAY I FEEL
(C'MON, BE HONEST - CIRCLE ONE)

I FEEL THIS WAY BECAUSE ...

-
-
-

TO FEEL MORE ENERGIZED I CAN ...
(WHAT PEOPLE OR ACTIVITIES GIVE YOU A BOOST?)

TODAY, MY TOP PROJECT IS ...

THIS PROJECT MATTERS TO ME BECAUSE ...

-

ONE SMALL ACTION I CAN TAKE TO MOVE FORWARD IS ...

-

OTHER THOUGHTS ...

TODAY, I'M GRATEFUL FOR ...

TODAY, I WILL STOP WORKING AT ...

_____ AM / PM

NOTES — PLAN THE DAY — BRAIN DUMP
(FREE SPACE TO HELP FREE YOUR MIND)

☀

6:00

7:00

8:00

9:00

10:00

11:00

12:00

1:00

2:00

3:00

4:00

5:00

6:00

7:00

8:00

☾

You're awesome! Go rock the day! 😉 👍 🚀 💥

TODAY I FEEL
(C'MON, BE HONEST - CIRCLE ONE)

I FEEL THIS WAY BECAUSE ...

-
-
-

TO FEEL MORE ENERGIZED I CAN ...
(WHAT PEOPLE OR ACTIVITIES GIVE YOU A BOOST?)

TODAY, MY TOP PROJECT IS ...

THIS PROJECT MATTERS TO ME BECAUSE ...

-

ONE SMALL ACTION I CAN TAKE TO MOVE FORWARD IS ...

-

OTHER THOUGHTS ...

TODAY, I'M GRATEFUL FOR ...

TODAY, I WILL STOP WORKING AT ...

_____ AM / PM

NOTES — PLAN THE DAY — BRAIN DUMP
(FREE SPACE TO HELP FREE YOUR MIND)

☀

6:00

7:00

8:00

9:00

10:00

11:00

12:00

1:00

2:00

3:00

4:00

5:00

6:00

7:00

8:00

☾

You're awesome! Go rock the day! 😅👍🚀💥

TIME    PLACE   DATE

TODAY I FEEL
(C'MON, BE HONEST - CIRCLE ONE)

Depleted   Meh   Fine   Good   Energized

I FEEL THIS WAY BECAUSE ...

-
-
-

TO FEEL MORE ENERGIZED I CAN ...
(WHAT PEOPLE OR ACTIVITIES GIVE YOU A BOOST?)

TODAY, MY TOP PROJECT IS ...

THIS PROJECT MATTERS TO ME BECAUSE ...

-

ONE SMALL ACTION I CAN TAKE TO MOVE FORWARD IS ...

-

OTHER THOUGHTS ...

TODAY, I'M GRATEFUL FOR ...

TODAY, I WILL STOP WORKING AT ...

_____ AM / PM

NOTES — PLAN THE DAY — BRAIN DUMP
(FREE SPACE TO HELP FREE YOUR MIND)

☀

6:00

7:00

8:00

9:00

10:00

11:00

12:00

1:00

2:00

3:00

4:00

5:00

6:00

7:00

8:00

☾

You're awesome! Go rock the day! 😌 👍 🚀 💥

TIME   📍 **PLACE**   **DATE**

TODAY I FEEL
(C'MON, BE HONEST - CIRCLE ONE)

I FEEL THIS WAY BECAUSE ...

-
-
-

TO FEEL MORE ENERGIZED I CAN ...
(WHAT PEOPLE OR ACTIVITIES GIVE YOU A BOOST?)

TODAY, MY TOP PROJECT IS ...

THIS PROJECT MATTERS TO ME BECAUSE ...

-

ONE SMALL ACTION I CAN TAKE TO MOVE FORWARD IS ...

-

OTHER THOUGHTS ...

TODAY, I'M GRATEFUL FOR ...

TODAY, I WILL STOP WORKING AT ...

_____ AM / PM

☀

6:00

7:00

8:00

9:00

10:00

11:00

12:00

1:00

2:00

3:00

4:00

5:00

6:00

7:00

8:00

☾

You're awesome! Go rock the day! 😊 👍 🚀 💥

TODAY I FEEL
(C'MON, BE HONEST - CIRCLE ONE)

I FEEL THIS WAY BECAUSE ...

-
-
-

TO FEEL MORE ENERGIZED I CAN ...
(WHAT PEOPLE OR ACTIVITIES GIVE YOU A BOOST?)

TODAY, MY TOP PROJECT IS ...

THIS PROJECT MATTERS TO ME BECAUSE ...

-

ONE SMALL ACTION I CAN TAKE TO MOVE FORWARD IS ...

-

OTHER THOUGHTS ...

TODAY, I'M GRATEFUL FOR ...

TODAY, I WILL STOP WORKING AT ...

_____ AM / PM

☀

6:00

7:00

8:00

9:00

10:00

11:00

12:00

1:00

2:00

3:00

4:00

5:00

6:00

7:00

8:00

☾

You're awesome! Go rock the day! 😉 👍 🚀 💥

TODAY I FEEL
(C'MON, BE HONEST - CIRCLE ONE)

I FEEL THIS WAY BECAUSE ...

-
-
-

TO FEEL MORE ENERGIZED I CAN ...
(WHAT PEOPLE OR ACTIVITIES GIVE YOU A BOOST?)

TODAY, MY TOP PROJECT IS ...

THIS PROJECT MATTERS TO ME BECAUSE ...

-

ONE SMALL ACTION I CAN TAKE TO MOVE FORWARD IS ...

-

OTHER THOUGHTS ...

TODAY, I'M GRATEFUL FOR ...

TODAY, I WILL STOP WORKING AT ...

_____ AM / PM

☀

6:00

7:00

8:00

9:00

10:00

11:00

12:00

1:00

2:00

3:00

4:00

5:00

6:00

7:00

8:00

☾

You're awesome! Go rock the day! 😄 👍 🚀 💥

TODAY I FEEL
(C'MON, BE HONEST - CIRCLE ONE)

I FEEL THIS WAY BECAUSE ...

-
-
-

TO FEEL MORE ENERGIZED I CAN ...
(WHAT PEOPLE OR ACTIVITIES GIVE YOU A BOOST?)

_____

_____

TODAY, MY TOP PROJECT IS ...

_____

_____

THIS PROJECT MATTERS TO ME BECAUSE ...

-

ONE SMALL ACTION I CAN TAKE TO MOVE FORWARD IS ...

-

OTHER THOUGHTS ...

_____

_____

_____

_____

_____

TODAY, I'M GRATEFUL FOR ...

_____

_____

TODAY, I WILL STOP WORKING AT ...

_____ AM / PM

☀

6:00

7:00

8:00

9:00

10:00

11:00

12:00

1:00

2:00

3:00

4:00

5:00

6:00

7:00

8:00

☾

You're awesome! Go rock the day! 😉 👍 🚀 💥

TODAY I FEEL
(C'MON, BE HONEST - CIRCLE ONE)

I FEEL THIS WAY BECAUSE ...

-
-
-

TO FEEL MORE ENERGIZED I CAN ...
(WHAT PEOPLE OR ACTIVITIES GIVE YOU A BOOST?)

TODAY, MY TOP PROJECT IS ...

THIS PROJECT MATTERS TO ME BECAUSE ...

-

ONE SMALL ACTION I CAN TAKE TO MOVE FORWARD IS ...

-

OTHER THOUGHTS ...

TODAY, I'M GRATEFUL FOR ...

TODAY, I WILL STOP WORKING AT ...

_____ AM / PM

☀

6:00

7:00

8:00

9:00

10:00

11:00

12:00

1:00

2:00

3:00

4:00

5:00

6:00

7:00

8:00

☾

You're awesome! Go rock the day! 😊 👍 🚀 💥

TODAY I FEEL
(C'MON, BE HONEST - CIRCLE ONE)

I FEEL THIS WAY BECAUSE ...

·

·

·

TO FEEL MORE ENERGIZED I CAN ...
(WHAT PEOPLE OR ACTIVITIES GIVE YOU A BOOST?)

TODAY, MY TOP PROJECT IS ...

THIS PROJECT MATTERS TO ME BECAUSE ...

·

ONE SMALL ACTION I CAN TAKE TO MOVE FORWARD IS ...

·

OTHER THOUGHTS ...

TODAY, I'M GRATEFUL FOR ...

TODAY, I WILL STOP WORKING AT ...

_____ AM / PM

☀

6:00

7:00

8:00

9:00

10:00

11:00

12:00

1:00

2:00

3:00

4:00

5:00

6:00

7:00

8:00

☾

You're awesome! Go rock the day! 😊 👍 🚀 💥

TODAY I FEEL
(C'MON, BE HONEST - CIRCLE ONE)

I FEEL THIS WAY BECAUSE ...

-
-
-

TO FEEL MORE ENERGIZED I CAN ...
(WHAT PEOPLE OR ACTIVITIES GIVE YOU A BOOST?)

TODAY, MY TOP PROJECT IS ...

THIS PROJECT MATTERS TO ME BECAUSE ...

-

ONE SMALL ACTION I CAN TAKE TO MOVE FORWARD IS ...

-

OTHER THOUGHTS ...

TODAY, I'M GRATEFUL FOR ...

TODAY, I WILL STOP WORKING AT ...

_____ AM / PM

NOTES — PLAN THE DAY — BRAIN DUMP
(FREE SPACE TO HELP FREE YOUR MIND)

☀

6:00

7:00

8:00

9:00

10:00

11:00

12:00

1:00

2:00

3:00

4:00

5:00

6:00

7:00

8:00

☾

You're awesome! Go rock the day! 😊 👍 🚀 💥

TODAY I FEEL
(C'MON, BE HONEST - CIRCLE ONE)

I FEEL THIS WAY BECAUSE ...

-
-
-

TO FEEL MORE ENERGIZED I CAN ...
(WHAT PEOPLE OR ACTIVITIES GIVE YOU A BOOST?)

TODAY, MY TOP PROJECT IS ...

THIS PROJECT MATTERS TO ME BECAUSE ...

-

ONE SMALL ACTION I CAN TAKE TO MOVE FORWARD IS ...

-

OTHER THOUGHTS ...

TODAY, I'M GRATEFUL FOR ...

TODAY, I WILL STOP WORKING AT ...

_____ AM / PM

NOTES — PLAN THE DAY — BRAIN DUMP

(FREE SPACE TO HELP FREE YOUR MIND)

☀

6:00

7:00

8:00

9:00

10:00

11:00

12:00

1:00

2:00

3:00

4:00

5:00

6:00

7:00

8:00

☾

You're awesome! Go rock the day! 😊 👍 🚀 💥

TODAY I FEEL
(C'MON, BE HONEST - CIRCLE ONE)

I FEEL THIS WAY BECAUSE ...

-
-
-

TO FEEL MORE ENERGIZED I CAN ...
(WHAT PEOPLE OR ACTIVITIES GIVE YOU A BOOST?)

TODAY, MY TOP PROJECT IS ...

THIS PROJECT MATTERS TO ME BECAUSE ...

-

ONE SMALL ACTION I CAN TAKE TO MOVE FORWARD IS ...

-

OTHER THOUGHTS ...

TODAY, I'M GRATEFUL FOR ...

TODAY, I WILL STOP WORKING AT ...

_____ AM / PM

☀

6:00

7:00

8:00

9:00

10:00

11:00

12:00

1:00

2:00

3:00

4:00

5:00

6:00

7:00

8:00

☾

You're awesome! Go rock the day! 😊 👍 🚀 💥

TODAY I FEEL

(C'MON, BE HONEST - CIRCLE ONE)

I FEEL THIS WAY BECAUSE ...

-
-
-

TO FEEL MORE ENERGIZED I CAN ...

(WHAT PEOPLE OR ACTIVITIES GIVE YOU A BOOST?)

TODAY, MY TOP PROJECT IS ...

THIS PROJECT MATTERS TO ME BECAUSE ...

-

ONE SMALL ACTION I CAN TAKE TO MOVE FORWARD IS ...

-

OTHER THOUGHTS ...

TODAY, I'M GRATEFUL FOR ...

TODAY, I WILL STOP WORKING AT ...

_____ AM / PM

NOTES — PLAN THE DAY — BRAIN DUMP

(FREE SPACE TO HELP FREE YOUR MIND)

☀

6:00

7:00

8:00

9:00

10:00

11:00

12:00

1:00

2:00

3:00

4:00

5:00

6:00

7:00

8:00

☾

You're awesome! Go rock the day! 😊 👍 🚀 💥

TIME　　　PLACE　　　　　　　　　DATE

TODAY I FEEL
(C'MON, BE HONEST - CIRCLE ONE)

I FEEL THIS WAY BECAUSE ...

-
-
-

TO FEEL MORE ENERGIZED I CAN ...
(WHAT PEOPLE OR ACTIVITIES GIVE YOU A BOOST?)

TODAY, MY TOP PROJECT IS ...

THIS PROJECT MATTERS TO ME BECAUSE ...

-

OTHER THOUGHTS ...

ONE SMALL ACTION I CAN TAKE TO MOVE FORWARD IS ...

-

TODAY, I'M GRATEFUL FOR ...

TODAY, I WILL STOP WORKING AT ...

_____ AM / PM

NOTES — PLAN THE DAY — BRAIN DUMP
(FREE SPACE TO HELP FREE YOUR MIND)

6:00

7:00

8:00

9:00

10:00

11:00

12:00

1:00

2:00

3:00

4:00

5:00

6:00

7:00

8:00

You're awesome! Go rock the day!

TODAY I FEEL
(C'MON, BE HONEST - CIRCLE ONE)

I FEEL THIS WAY BECAUSE ...

-
-
-

TO FEEL MORE ENERGIZED I CAN ...
(WHAT PEOPLE OR ACTIVITIES GIVE YOU A BOOST?)

_____

_____

TODAY, MY TOP PROJECT IS ...

_____

THIS PROJECT MATTERS TO ME BECAUSE ...

-

ONE SMALL ACTION I CAN TAKE TO MOVE FORWARD IS ...

-

OTHER THOUGHTS ...

_____

_____

_____

_____

_____

TODAY, I'M GRATEFUL FOR ...

_____

_____

TODAY, I WILL STOP WORKING AT ...

_____ AM / PM

☀

6:00

7:00

8:00

9:00

10:00

11:00

12:00

1:00

2:00

3:00

4:00

5:00

6:00

7:00

8:00

☾

You're awesome! Go rock the day! 😉 👍 🚀 💥

TODAY I FEEL
(C'MON, BE HONEST - CIRCLE ONE)

I FEEL THIS WAY BECAUSE ...

-
-
-

TO FEEL MORE ENERGIZED I CAN ...
(WHAT PEOPLE OR ACTIVITIES GIVE YOU A BOOST?)

_____

_____

TODAY, MY TOP PROJECT IS ...

_____

_____

THIS PROJECT MATTERS TO ME BECAUSE ...

-

ONE SMALL ACTION I CAN TAKE TO MOVE FORWARD IS ...

-

OTHER THOUGHTS ...

_____
_____
_____
_____
_____
_____

TODAY, I'M GRATEFUL FOR ...

_____
_____

TODAY, I WILL STOP WORKING AT ...

_____ AM / PM

NOTES — PLAN THE DAY — BRAIN DUMP
(FREE SPACE TO HELP FREE YOUR MIND)

☀

6:00

7:00

8:00

9:00

10:00

11:00

12:00

1:00

2:00

3:00

4:00

5:00

6:00

7:00

8:00

☾

You're awesome! Go rock the day! 😊 👍 🚀 💥

TODAY I FEEL
(C'MON, BE HONEST - CIRCLE ONE)

I FEEL THIS WAY BECAUSE ...

-
-
-

TO FEEL MORE ENERGIZED I CAN ...
(WHAT PEOPLE OR ACTIVITIES GIVE YOU A BOOST?)

_____

_____

TODAY, MY TOP PROJECT IS ...

_____

_____

THIS PROJECT MATTERS TO ME BECAUSE ...

-

ONE SMALL ACTION I CAN TAKE TO MOVE FORWARD IS ...

-

OTHER THOUGHTS ...

_____

_____

_____

_____

_____

TODAY, I'M GRATEFUL FOR ...

_____

_____

TODAY, I WILL STOP WORKING AT ...

_____ AM / PM

NOTES — PLAN THE DAY — BRAIN DUMP

(FREE SPACE TO HELP FREE YOUR MIND)

☀

6:00

7:00

8:00

9:00

10:00

11:00

12:00

1:00

2:00

3:00

4:00

5:00

6:00

7:00

8:00

☾

You're awesome! Go rock the day! 😌 👍 🚀 💥

TODAY I FEEL
(C'MON, BE HONEST - CIRCLE ONE)

I FEEL THIS WAY BECAUSE ...

-
-
-

TO FEEL MORE ENERGIZED I CAN ...
(WHAT PEOPLE OR ACTIVITIES GIVE YOU A BOOST?)

_____

_____

TODAY, MY TOP PROJECT IS ...

_____

_____

THIS PROJECT MATTERS TO ME BECAUSE ...

-

ONE SMALL ACTION I CAN TAKE TO MOVE FORWARD IS ...

-

OTHER THOUGHTS ...

_____
_____
_____
_____
_____

TODAY, I'M GRATEFUL FOR ...

_____
_____

TODAY, I WILL STOP WORKING AT ...

_____ AM / PM

NOTES — PLAN THE DAY — BRAIN DUMP

(FREE SPACE TO HELP FREE YOUR MIND)

☀

6:00

7:00

8:00

9:00

10:00

11:00

12:00

1:00

2:00

3:00

4:00

5:00

6:00

7:00

8:00

☾

You're awesome! Go rock the day! 😴 👍 🚀 💥

TODAY I FEEL
(C'MON, BE HONEST - CIRCLE ONE)

I FEEL THIS WAY BECAUSE ...

-
-
-

TO FEEL MORE ENERGIZED I CAN ...
(WHAT PEOPLE OR ACTIVITIES GIVE YOU A BOOST?)

_____

_____

TODAY, MY TOP PROJECT IS ...

_____

_____

THIS PROJECT MATTERS TO ME BECAUSE ...

-

ONE SMALL ACTION I CAN TAKE TO MOVE FORWARD IS ...

-

OTHER THOUGHTS ...

_____
_____
_____
_____
_____
_____

TODAY, I'M GRATEFUL FOR ...

_____

_____

TODAY, I WILL STOP WORKING AT ...

_____ AM / PM

NOTES — PLAN THE DAY — BRAIN DUMP

(FREE SPACE TO HELP FREE YOUR MIND)

☀

6:00

7:00

8:00

9:00

10:00

11:00

12:00

1:00

2:00

3:00

4:00

5:00

6:00

7:00

8:00

☾

You're awesome! Go rock the day! 😊 👍 🚀 💥

TODAY I FEEL
(C'MON, BE HONEST - CIRCLE ONE)

I FEEL THIS WAY BECAUSE ...

-
-
-

TO FEEL MORE ENERGIZED I CAN ...
(WHAT PEOPLE OR ACTIVITIES GIVE YOU A BOOST?)

TODAY, MY TOP PROJECT IS ...

THIS PROJECT MATTERS TO ME BECAUSE ...

-

ONE SMALL ACTION I CAN TAKE TO MOVE FORWARD IS ...

-

OTHER THOUGHTS ...

TODAY, I'M GRATEFUL FOR ...

TODAY, I WILL STOP WORKING AT ...

_____ AM / PM

NOTES — PLAN THE DAY — BRAIN DUMP
(FREE SPACE TO HELP FREE YOUR MIND)

☀

6:00

7:00

8:00

9:00

10:00

11:00

12:00

1:00

2:00

3:00

4:00

5:00

6:00

7:00

8:00

☾

You're awesome! Go rock the day! 😊 👍 🚀 💥

TODAY I FEEL
(C'MON, BE HONEST - CIRCLE ONE)

I FEEL THIS WAY BECAUSE ...

-
-
-

TO FEEL MORE ENERGIZED I CAN ...
(WHAT PEOPLE OR ACTIVITIES GIVE YOU A BOOST?)

TODAY, MY TOP PROJECT IS ...

THIS PROJECT MATTERS TO ME BECAUSE ...

-

ONE SMALL ACTION I CAN TAKE TO MOVE FORWARD IS ...

-

OTHER THOUGHTS ...

TODAY, I'M GRATEFUL FOR ...

TODAY, I WILL STOP WORKING AT ...

_____ AM / PM

☀

6:00

7:00

8:00

9:00

10:00

11:00

12:00

1:00

2:00

3:00

4:00

5:00

6:00

7:00

8:00

☾

You're awesome! Go rock the day! 😊 👍 🚀 💥

TODAY I FEEL
(C'MON, BE HONEST - CIRCLE ONE)

I FEEL THIS WAY BECAUSE ...

-
-
-

TO FEEL MORE ENERGIZED I CAN ...
(WHAT PEOPLE OR ACTIVITIES GIVE YOU A BOOST?)

_____

_____

TODAY, MY TOP PROJECT IS ...

_____

_____

THIS PROJECT MATTERS TO ME BECAUSE ...

-

ONE SMALL ACTION I CAN TAKE TO MOVE FORWARD IS ...

-

OTHER THOUGHTS ...

_____

_____

_____

_____

_____

_____

TODAY, I'M GRATEFUL FOR ...

_____

_____

TODAY, I WILL STOP WORKING AT ...

_____ AM / PM

NOTES — PLAN THE DAY — BRAIN DUMP
(FREE SPACE TO HELP FREE YOUR MIND)

☀

6:00

7:00

8:00

9:00

10:00

11:00

12:00

1:00

2:00

3:00

4:00

5:00

6:00

7:00

8:00

☾

You're awesome! Go rock the day! 😌 👍 🚀 💥

TODAY I FEEL
(C'MON, BE HONEST - CIRCLE ONE)

I FEEL THIS WAY BECAUSE ...

-
-
-

TO FEEL MORE ENERGIZED I CAN ...
(WHAT PEOPLE OR ACTIVITIES GIVE YOU A BOOST?)

TODAY, MY TOP PROJECT IS ...

THIS PROJECT MATTERS TO ME BECAUSE ...

-

ONE SMALL ACTION I CAN TAKE TO MOVE FORWARD IS ...

-

OTHER THOUGHTS ...

TODAY, I'M GRATEFUL FOR ...

TODAY, I WILL STOP WORKING AT ...

_____ AM / PM

NOTES — PLAN THE DAY — BRAIN DUMP
(FREE SPACE TO HELP FREE YOUR MIND)

☀

6:00

7:00

8:00

9:00

10:00

11:00

12:00

1:00

2:00

3:00

4:00

5:00

6:00

7:00

8:00

☾

You're awesome! Go rock the day! 😉 👍 🚀 💥

TODAY I FEEL
(C'MON, BE HONEST - CIRCLE ONE)

I FEEL THIS WAY BECAUSE ...

-
-
-

TO FEEL MORE ENERGIZED I CAN ...
(WHAT PEOPLE OR ACTIVITIES GIVE YOU A BOOST?)

TODAY, MY TOP PROJECT IS ...

THIS PROJECT MATTERS TO ME BECAUSE ...

-

ONE SMALL ACTION I CAN TAKE TO MOVE FORWARD IS ...

-

OTHER THOUGHTS ...

TODAY, I'M GRATEFUL FOR ...

TODAY, I WILL STOP WORKING AT ...

_____ AM / PM

NOTES — PLAN THE DAY — BRAIN DUMP

(FREE SPACE TO HELP FREE YOUR MIND)

☀

6:00

7:00

8:00

9:00

10:00

11:00

12:00

1:00

2:00

3:00

4:00

5:00

6:00

7:00

8:00

☾

You're awesome! Go rock the day! 😊 👍 🚀 💥

TODAY I FEEL
(C'MON, BE HONEST - CIRCLE ONE)

I FEEL THIS WAY BECAUSE ...

-
-
-

TO FEEL MORE ENERGIZED I CAN ...
(WHAT PEOPLE OR ACTIVITIES GIVE YOU A BOOST?)

_____

_____

TODAY, MY TOP PROJECT IS ...

_____

_____

THIS PROJECT MATTERS TO ME BECAUSE ...

-

ONE SMALL ACTION I CAN TAKE TO MOVE FORWARD IS ...

-

OTHER THOUGHTS ...

_____

_____

_____

_____

TODAY, I'M GRATEFUL FOR ...

_____

_____

TODAY, I WILL STOP WORKING AT ...

_____ AM / PM

NOTES — PLAN THE DAY — BRAIN DUMP
(FREE SPACE TO HELP FREE YOUR MIND)

☀

6:00

7:00

8:00

9:00

10:00

11:00

12:00

1:00

2:00

3:00

4:00

5:00

6:00

7:00

8:00

☾

You're awesome! Go rock the day! 😊 👍 🚀 💥

TODAY I FEEL
(C'MON, BE HONEST - CIRCLE ONE)

I FEEL THIS WAY BECAUSE ...

-
-
-

TO FEEL MORE ENERGIZED I CAN ...
(WHAT PEOPLE OR ACTIVITIES GIVE YOU A BOOST?)

TODAY, MY TOP PROJECT IS ...

THIS PROJECT MATTERS TO ME BECAUSE ...

-

ONE SMALL ACTION I CAN TAKE TO MOVE FORWARD IS ...

-

OTHER THOUGHTS ...

TODAY, I'M GRATEFUL FOR ...

TODAY, I WILL STOP WORKING AT ...

_____ AM / PM

☀️

6:00

7:00

8:00

9:00

10:00

11:00

12:00

1:00

2:00

3:00

4:00

5:00

6:00

7:00

8:00

☾

You're awesome! Go rock the day! 😉 👍 🚀 💥

TODAY I FEEL
(C'MON, BE HONEST - CIRCLE ONE)

I FEEL THIS WAY BECAUSE ...

-
-
-

TO FEEL MORE ENERGIZED I CAN ...
(WHAT PEOPLE OR ACTIVITIES GIVE YOU A BOOST?)

_____

_____

TODAY, MY TOP PROJECT IS ...

_____

THIS PROJECT MATTERS TO ME BECAUSE ...

-

ONE SMALL ACTION I CAN TAKE TO MOVE FORWARD IS ...

-

OTHER THOUGHTS ...

_____
_____
_____
_____
_____
_____

TODAY, I'M GRATEFUL FOR ...

_____
_____

TODAY, I WILL STOP WORKING AT ...

_____ AM / PM

NOTES — PLAN THE DAY — BRAIN DUMP

(FREE SPACE TO HELP FREE YOUR MIND)

☀

6:00

7:00

8:00

9:00

10:00

11:00

12:00

1:00

2:00

3:00

4:00

5:00

6:00

7:00

8:00

☾

You're awesome! Go rock the day! 😊 👍 🚀 💥

TODAY I FEEL
(C'MON, BE HONEST - CIRCLE ONE)

I FEEL THIS WAY BECAUSE ...

-
-
-

TO FEEL MORE ENERGIZED I CAN ...
(WHAT PEOPLE OR ACTIVITIES GIVE YOU A BOOST?)

TODAY, MY TOP PROJECT IS ...

THIS PROJECT MATTERS TO ME BECAUSE ...

-

ONE SMALL ACTION I CAN TAKE TO MOVE FORWARD IS ...

-

OTHER THOUGHTS ...

TODAY, I'M GRATEFUL FOR ...

TODAY, I WILL STOP WORKING AT ...

_____ AM / PM

NOTES — PLAN THE DAY — BRAIN DUMP
(FREE SPACE TO HELP FREE YOUR MIND)

☀

6:00

7:00

8:00

9:00

10:00

11:00

12:00

1:00

2:00

3:00

4:00

5:00

6:00

7:00

8:00

☾

You're awesome! Go rock the day! 😊 👍 🚀 💥

TODAY I FEEL
(C'MON, BE HONEST - CIRCLE ONE)

I FEEL THIS WAY BECAUSE ...

-
-
-

TO FEEL MORE ENERGIZED I CAN ...
(WHAT PEOPLE OR ACTIVITIES GIVE YOU A BOOST?)

_____

_____

TODAY, MY TOP PROJECT IS ...

_____

_____

THIS PROJECT MATTERS TO ME BECAUSE ...

-

ONE SMALL ACTION I CAN TAKE TO MOVE FORWARD IS ...

-

OTHER THOUGHTS ...

_____

_____

_____

_____

TODAY, I'M GRATEFUL FOR ...

_____

_____

TODAY, I WILL STOP WORKING AT ...

_____ AM / PM

☀

6:00

7:00

8:00

9:00

10:00

11:00

12:00

1:00

2:00

3:00

4:00

5:00

6:00

7:00

8:00

☾

You're awesome! Go rock the day! 😊 👍 🚀 💥

TODAY I FEEL
(C'MON, BE HONEST - CIRCLE ONE)

I FEEL THIS WAY BECAUSE ...

-
-
-

TO FEEL MORE ENERGIZED I CAN ...
(WHAT PEOPLE OR ACTIVITIES GIVE YOU A BOOST?)

_____

_____

TODAY, MY TOP PROJECT IS ...

_____

_____

THIS PROJECT MATTERS TO ME BECAUSE ...

-

ONE SMALL ACTION I CAN TAKE TO MOVE FORWARD IS ...

-

OTHER THOUGHTS ...

_____

_____

_____

_____

_____

TODAY, I'M GRATEFUL FOR ...

_____

TODAY, I WILL STOP WORKING AT ...

_____ AM / PM

NOTES — PLAN THE DAY — BRAIN DUMP
(FREE SPACE TO HELP FREE YOUR MIND)

☀

6:00

7:00

8:00

9:00

10:00

11:00

12:00

1:00

2:00

3:00

4:00

5:00

6:00

7:00

8:00

☾

You're awesome! Go rock the day! 😊 👍 🚀 💥

TODAY I FEEL
(C'MON, BE HONEST - CIRCLE ONE)

I FEEL THIS WAY BECAUSE ...

-
-
-

TO FEEL MORE ENERGIZED I CAN ...
(WHAT PEOPLE OR ACTIVITIES GIVE YOU A BOOST?)

_____

_____

TODAY, MY TOP PROJECT IS ...

_____

_____

THIS PROJECT MATTERS TO ME BECAUSE ...

-

ONE SMALL ACTION I CAN TAKE TO MOVE FORWARD IS ...

-

OTHER THOUGHTS ...

_____
_____
_____
_____
_____
_____

TODAY, I'M GRATEFUL FOR ...

_____

TODAY, I WILL STOP WORKING AT ...

_____ AM / PM

☀

6:00

7:00

8:00

9:00

10:00

11:00

12:00

1:00

2:00

3:00

4:00

5:00

6:00

7:00

8:00

☾

You're awesome! Go rock the day! 😊 👍 🚀 💥

TODAY I FEEL
(C'MON, BE HONEST - CIRCLE ONE)

I FEEL THIS WAY BECAUSE …

-
-
-

TO FEEL MORE ENERGIZED I CAN …
(WHAT PEOPLE OR ACTIVITIES GIVE YOU A BOOST?)

_____

_____

TODAY, MY TOP PROJECT IS …

_____

_____

THIS PROJECT MATTERS TO ME BECAUSE …

-

ONE SMALL ACTION I CAN TAKE TO MOVE FORWARD IS …

-

OTHER THOUGHTS …

_____

_____

_____

_____

_____

TODAY, I'M GRATEFUL FOR …

_____

_____

TODAY, I WILL STOP WORKING AT …

_____ AM / PM

☀

6:00

7:00

8:00

9:00

10:00

11:00

12:00

1:00

2:00

3:00

4:00

5:00

6:00

7:00

8:00

☾

You're awesome! Go rock the day! 😉 👍 🚀 💥

TODAY I FEEL
(C'MON, BE HONEST - CIRCLE ONE)

I FEEL THIS WAY BECAUSE ...

-
-
-

TO FEEL MORE ENERGIZED I CAN ...
(WHAT PEOPLE OR ACTIVITIES GIVE YOU A BOOST?)

TODAY, MY TOP PROJECT IS ...

THIS PROJECT MATTERS TO ME BECAUSE ...

-

ONE SMALL ACTION I CAN TAKE TO MOVE FORWARD IS ...

-

OTHER THOUGHTS ...

TODAY, I'M GRATEFUL FOR ...

TODAY, I WILL STOP WORKING AT ...

_____ AM / PM

☀

6:00

7:00

8:00

9:00

10:00

11:00

12:00

1:00

2:00

3:00

4:00

5:00

6:00

7:00

8:00

☾

You're awesome! Go rock the day! 😟 👍 🚀 💥

TODAY I FEEL
(C'MON, BE HONEST - CIRCLE ONE)

I FEEL THIS WAY BECAUSE ...

-
-
-

TO FEEL MORE ENERGIZED I CAN ...
(WHAT PEOPLE OR ACTIVITIES GIVE YOU A BOOST?)

TODAY, MY TOP PROJECT IS ...

THIS PROJECT MATTERS TO ME BECAUSE ...

-

ONE SMALL ACTION I CAN TAKE TO MOVE FORWARD IS ...

-

OTHER THOUGHTS ...

TODAY, I'M GRATEFUL FOR ...

TODAY, I WILL STOP WORKING AT ...

_____ AM / PM

☀

6:00

7:00

8:00

9:00

10:00

11:00

12:00

1:00

2:00

3:00

4:00

5:00

6:00

7:00

8:00

☾

You're awesome! Go rock the day! 😉 👍 🚀 💥

TODAY I FEEL
(C'MON, BE HONEST - CIRCLE ONE)

I FEEL THIS WAY BECAUSE ...

-
-
-

TO FEEL MORE ENERGIZED I CAN ...
(WHAT PEOPLE OR ACTIVITIES GIVE YOU A BOOST?)

TODAY, MY TOP PROJECT IS ...

THIS PROJECT MATTERS TO ME BECAUSE ...

-

ONE SMALL ACTION I CAN TAKE TO MOVE FORWARD IS ...

-

OTHER THOUGHTS ...

TODAY, I'M GRATEFUL FOR ...

TODAY, I WILL STOP WORKING AT ...

_____ AM / PM

☀

6:00

7:00

8:00

9:00

10:00

11:00

12:00

1:00

2:00

3:00

4:00

5:00

6:00

7:00

8:00

☾

You're awesome! Go rock the day! 😊👍🚀💥

TODAY I FEEL
(C'MON, BE HONEST - CIRCLE ONE)

I FEEL THIS WAY BECAUSE ...

-
-
-

TO FEEL MORE ENERGIZED I CAN ...
(WHAT PEOPLE OR ACTIVITIES GIVE YOU A BOOST?)

_____

_____

TODAY, MY TOP PROJECT IS ...

_____

_____

THIS PROJECT MATTERS TO ME BECAUSE ...

-

ONE SMALL ACTION I CAN TAKE TO MOVE FORWARD IS ...

-

OTHER THOUGHTS ...

_____
_____
_____
_____
_____

TODAY, I'M GRATEFUL FOR ...

TODAY, I WILL STOP WORKING AT ...

_____ AM / PM

☀

6:00

7:00

8:00

9:00

10:00

11:00

12:00

1:00

2:00

3:00

4:00

5:00

6:00

7:00

8:00

☾

You're awesome! Go rock the day! 😊 👍 🚀 💥

TODAY I FEEL
(C'MON, BE HONEST - CIRCLE ONE)

Depleted   Meh   Fine   Good   Energized

I FEEL THIS WAY BECAUSE ...

-
-
-

TO FEEL MORE ENERGIZED I CAN ...
(WHAT PEOPLE OR ACTIVITIES GIVE YOU A BOOST?)

TODAY, MY TOP PROJECT IS ...

THIS PROJECT MATTERS TO ME BECAUSE ...

-

ONE SMALL ACTION I CAN TAKE TO MOVE FORWARD IS ...

-

OTHER THOUGHTS ...

TODAY, I'M GRATEFUL FOR ...

TODAY, I WILL STOP WORKING AT ...

_____ AM / PM

☀

6:00

7:00

8:00

9:00

10:00

11:00

12:00

1:00

2:00

3:00

4:00

5:00

6:00

7:00

8:00

☾

You're awesome! Go rock the day! 😊👍🚀💥

TODAY I FEEL
(C'MON, BE HONEST - CIRCLE ONE)

I FEEL THIS WAY BECAUSE …

-
-
-

TO FEEL MORE ENERGIZED I CAN …
(WHAT PEOPLE OR ACTIVITIES GIVE YOU A BOOST?)

_____

_____

TODAY, MY TOP PROJECT IS …

_____

_____

THIS PROJECT MATTERS TO ME BECAUSE …

-

ONE SMALL ACTION I CAN TAKE TO MOVE FORWARD IS …

-

OTHER THOUGHTS …

_____
_____
_____
_____
_____

TODAY, I'M GRATEFUL FOR …

_____
_____

TODAY, I WILL STOP WORKING AT …

_____ AM / PM

☀

6:00

7:00

8:00

9:00

10:00

11:00

12:00

1:00

2:00

3:00

4:00

5:00

6:00

7:00

8:00

☾

You're awesome! Go rock the day! 😌 👍 🚀 💥

TODAY I FEEL
(C'MON, BE HONEST - CIRCLE ONE)

I FEEL THIS WAY BECAUSE …

-
-
-

TO FEEL MORE ENERGIZED I CAN …
(WHAT PEOPLE OR ACTIVITIES GIVE YOU A BOOST?)

TODAY, MY TOP PROJECT IS …

THIS PROJECT MATTERS TO ME BECAUSE …

-

ONE SMALL ACTION I CAN TAKE TO MOVE FORWARD IS …

-

OTHER THOUGHTS …

TODAY, I'M GRATEFUL FOR …

TODAY, I WILL STOP WORKING AT …

_____ AM / PM

☀

6:00

7:00

8:00

9:00

10:00

11:00

12:00

1:00

2:00

3:00

4:00

5:00

6:00

7:00

8:00

☾

You're awesome! Go rock the day!   😊 👍 🚀 💥

TODAY I FEEL
(C'MON, BE HONEST - CIRCLE ONE)

I FEEL THIS WAY BECAUSE …

-
-
-

TO FEEL MORE ENERGIZED I CAN …
(WHAT PEOPLE OR ACTIVITIES GIVE YOU A BOOST?)

TODAY, MY TOP PROJECT IS …

THIS PROJECT MATTERS TO ME BECAUSE …

-

ONE SMALL ACTION I CAN TAKE TO MOVE FORWARD IS …

-

OTHER THOUGHTS …

TODAY, I'M GRATEFUL FOR …

TODAY, I WILL STOP WORKING AT …

_____ AM / PM

246

☀

6:00

7:00

8:00

9:00

10:00

11:00

12:00

1:00

2:00

3:00

4:00

5:00

6:00

7:00

8:00

☾

You're awesome! Go rock the day! 😊 👍 🚀 💥

TODAY I FEEL
(C'MON, BE HONEST - CIRCLE ONE)

I FEEL THIS WAY BECAUSE …

-
-
-

TO FEEL MORE ENERGIZED I CAN …
(WHAT PEOPLE OR ACTIVITIES GIVE YOU A BOOST?)

_____

_____

TODAY, MY TOP PROJECT IS …

_____

_____

THIS PROJECT MATTERS TO ME BECAUSE …

-

ONE SMALL ACTION I CAN TAKE TO MOVE FORWARD IS …

-

OTHER THOUGHTS …

_____
_____
_____
_____
_____

TODAY, I'M GRATEFUL FOR …

_____

TODAY, I WILL STOP WORKING AT …

_____ AM / PM

☀

6:00

7:00

8:00

9:00

10:00

11:00

12:00

1:00

2:00

3:00

4:00

5:00

6:00

7:00

8:00

☾

You're awesome! Go rock the day! 😊 👍 🚀 💥

TODAY I FEEL
(C'MON, BE HONEST - CIRCLE ONE)

I FEEL THIS WAY BECAUSE ...

-
-
-

TO FEEL MORE ENERGIZED I CAN ...
(WHAT PEOPLE OR ACTIVITIES GIVE YOU A BOOST?)

TODAY, MY TOP PROJECT IS ...

THIS PROJECT MATTERS TO ME BECAUSE ...

-

ONE SMALL ACTION I CAN TAKE TO MOVE FORWARD IS ...

-

OTHER THOUGHTS ...

TODAY, I'M GRATEFUL FOR ...

TODAY, I WILL STOP WORKING AT ...

_____ AM / PM

NOTES — PLAN THE DAY — BRAIN DUMP
(FREE SPACE TO HELP FREE YOUR MIND)

☀

6:00

7:00

8:00

9:00

10:00

11:00

12:00

1:00

2:00

3:00

4:00

5:00

6:00

7:00

8:00

☾

You're awesome! Go rock the day! 😊 👍 🚀 💥

TODAY I FEEL
(C'MON, BE HONEST - CIRCLE ONE)

I FEEL THIS WAY BECAUSE ...

-
-
-

TO FEEL MORE ENERGIZED I CAN ...
(WHAT PEOPLE OR ACTIVITIES GIVE YOU A BOOST?)

TODAY, MY TOP PROJECT IS ...

THIS PROJECT MATTERS TO ME BECAUSE ...

-

ONE SMALL ACTION I CAN TAKE TO MOVE FORWARD IS ...

-

OTHER THOUGHTS ...

TODAY, I'M GRATEFUL FOR ...

TODAY, I WILL STOP WORKING AT ...

_____ AM / PM

☀

6:00

7:00

8:00

9:00

10:00

11:00

12:00

1:00

2:00

3:00

4:00

5:00

6:00

7:00

8:00

☾

You're awesome! Go rock the day! 😊 👍 🚀 💥

TODAY I FEEL
(C'MON, BE HONEST - CIRCLE ONE)

I FEEL THIS WAY BECAUSE ...

-
-
-

TO FEEL MORE ENERGIZED I CAN ...
(WHAT PEOPLE OR ACTIVITIES GIVE YOU A BOOST?)

TODAY, MY TOP PROJECT IS ...

THIS PROJECT MATTERS TO ME BECAUSE ...

-

ONE SMALL ACTION I CAN TAKE TO MOVE FORWARD IS ...

-

OTHER THOUGHTS ...

TODAY, I'M GRATEFUL FOR ...

TODAY, I WILL STOP WORKING AT ...

_____ AM / PM

☀️

6:00

7:00

8:00

9:00

10:00

11:00

12:00

1:00

2:00

3:00

4:00

5:00

6:00

7:00

8:00

🌙

You're awesome! Go rock the day! 😌 👍 🚀 💥

TODAY I FEEL
(C'MON, BE HONEST - CIRCLE ONE)

I FEEL THIS WAY BECAUSE ...

-
-
-

TO FEEL MORE ENERGIZED I CAN ...
(WHAT PEOPLE OR ACTIVITIES GIVE YOU A BOOST?)

TODAY, MY TOP PROJECT IS ...

THIS PROJECT MATTERS TO ME BECAUSE ...

-

ONE SMALL ACTION I CAN TAKE TO MOVE FORWARD IS ...

-

OTHER THOUGHTS ...

TODAY, I'M GRATEFUL FOR ...

TODAY, I WILL STOP WORKING AT ...

_____ AM / PM

☀

6:00

7:00

8:00

9:00

10:00

11:00

12:00

1:00

2:00

3:00

4:00

5:00

6:00

7:00

8:00

☾

You're awesome! Go rock the day! 😉 👍 🚀 💥

TODAY I FEEL
(C'MON, BE HONEST - CIRCLE ONE)

I FEEL THIS WAY BECAUSE ...

-
-
-

TO FEEL MORE ENERGIZED I CAN ...
(WHAT PEOPLE OR ACTIVITIES GIVE YOU A BOOST?)

TODAY, MY TOP PROJECT IS ...

THIS PROJECT MATTERS TO ME BECAUSE ...

-

ONE SMALL ACTION I CAN TAKE TO MOVE FORWARD IS ...

-

OTHER THOUGHTS ...

TODAY, I'M GRATEFUL FOR ...

TODAY, I WILL STOP WORKING AT ...

_____ AM / PM

NOTES — PLAN THE DAY — BRAIN DUMP
(FREE SPACE TO HELP FREE YOUR MIND)

☀

6:00

7:00

8:00

9:00

10:00

11:00

12:00

1:00

2:00

3:00

4:00

5:00

6:00

7:00

8:00

☾

You're awesome! Go rock the day! 😊 👍 🚀 💥

TODAY I FEEL
(C'MON, BE HONEST - CIRCLE ONE)

I FEEL THIS WAY BECAUSE ...

-
-
-

TO FEEL MORE ENERGIZED I CAN ...
(WHAT PEOPLE OR ACTIVITIES GIVE YOU A BOOST?)

TODAY, MY TOP PROJECT IS ...

THIS PROJECT MATTERS TO ME BECAUSE ...

-

ONE SMALL ACTION I CAN TAKE TO MOVE FORWARD IS ...

-

OTHER THOUGHTS ...

TODAY, I'M GRATEFUL FOR ...

TODAY, I WILL STOP WORKING AT ...

_____ AM / PM

NOTES — PLAN THE DAY — BRAIN DUMP
(FREE SPACE TO HELP FREE YOUR MIND)

☀

6:00

7:00

8:00

9:00

10:00

11:00

12:00

1:00

2:00

3:00

4:00

5:00

6:00

7:00

8:00

☾

You're awesome! Go rock the day! 😊 👍 🚀 💥

TODAY I FEEL
(C'MON, BE HONEST - CIRCLE ONE)

I FEEL THIS WAY BECAUSE ...

-
-
-

TO FEEL MORE ENERGIZED I CAN ...
(WHAT PEOPLE OR ACTIVITIES GIVE YOU A BOOST?)

TODAY, MY TOP PROJECT IS ...

THIS PROJECT MATTERS TO ME BECAUSE ...

-

ONE SMALL ACTION I CAN TAKE TO MOVE FORWARD IS ...

-

OTHER THOUGHTS ...

TODAY, I'M GRATEFUL FOR ...

TODAY, I WILL STOP WORKING AT ...

_____ AM / PM

NOTES — PLAN THE DAY — BRAIN DUMP

(FREE SPACE TO HELP FREE YOUR MIND)

☀

6:00

7:00

8:00

9:00

10:00

11:00

12:00

1:00

2:00

3:00

4:00

5:00

6:00

7:00

8:00

☾

You're awesome! Go rock the day! 😊 👍 🚀 💥

TODAY I FEEL
(C'MON, BE HONEST - CIRCLE ONE)

I FEEL THIS WAY BECAUSE ...

-
-
-

TO FEEL MORE ENERGIZED I CAN ...
(WHAT PEOPLE OR ACTIVITIES GIVE YOU A BOOST?)

TODAY, MY TOP PROJECT IS ...

THIS PROJECT MATTERS TO ME BECAUSE ...

-

ONE SMALL ACTION I CAN TAKE TO MOVE FORWARD IS ...

-

OTHER THOUGHTS ...

TODAY, I'M GRATEFUL FOR ...

TODAY, I WILL STOP WORKING AT ...

_____ AM / PM

NOTES — PLAN THE DAY — BRAIN DUMP

(FREE SPACE TO HELP FREE YOUR MIND)

☀

6:00

7:00

8:00

9:00

10:00

11:00

12:00

1:00

2:00

3:00

4:00

5:00

6:00

7:00

8:00

☾

You're awesome! Go rock the day! 😋 👍 🚀 💥

TODAY I FEEL
(C'MON, BE HONEST - CIRCLE ONE)

I FEEL THIS WAY BECAUSE ...

-
-
-

TO FEEL MORE ENERGIZED I CAN ...
(WHAT PEOPLE OR ACTIVITIES GIVE YOU A BOOST?)

TODAY, MY TOP PROJECT IS ...

THIS PROJECT MATTERS TO ME BECAUSE ...

-

ONE SMALL ACTION I CAN TAKE TO MOVE FORWARD IS ...

-

OTHER THOUGHTS ...

TODAY, I'M GRATEFUL FOR ...

TODAY, I WILL STOP WORKING AT ...

_____ AM / PM

NOTES — PLAN THE DAY — BRAIN DUMP
(FREE SPACE TO HELP FREE YOUR MIND)

☀

6:00

7:00

8:00

9:00

10:00

11:00

12:00

1:00

2:00

3:00

4:00

5:00

6:00

7:00

8:00

☾

You're awesome! Go rock the day! 😊 👍 🚀 💥

TODAY I FEEL
(C'MON, BE HONEST - CIRCLE ONE)

I FEEL THIS WAY BECAUSE ...

-
-
-

TO FEEL MORE ENERGIZED I CAN ...
(WHAT PEOPLE OR ACTIVITIES GIVE YOU A BOOST?)

_____

_____

TODAY, MY TOP PROJECT IS ...

_____

_____

THIS PROJECT MATTERS TO ME BECAUSE ...

-

ONE SMALL ACTION I CAN TAKE TO MOVE FORWARD IS ...

-

OTHER THOUGHTS ...

_____
_____
_____
_____
_____

TODAY, I'M GRATEFUL FOR ...

_____

TODAY, I WILL STOP WORKING AT ...

_____ AM / PM

NOTES — PLAN THE DAY — BRAIN DUMP

(FREE SPACE TO HELP FREE YOUR MIND)

☀

6:00

7:00

8:00

9:00

10:00

11:00

12:00

1:00

2:00

3:00

4:00

5:00

6:00

7:00

8:00

☾

You're awesome! Go rock the day! 😊 👍 🚀 💥

TODAY I FEEL
(C'MON, BE HONEST - CIRCLE ONE)

I FEEL THIS WAY BECAUSE ...

- •
- •
- •

TO FEEL MORE ENERGIZED I CAN ...
(WHAT PEOPLE OR ACTIVITIES GIVE YOU A BOOST?)

_____

_____

TODAY, MY TOP PROJECT IS ...

_____

_____

THIS PROJECT MATTERS TO ME BECAUSE ...

- •

ONE SMALL ACTION I CAN TAKE TO MOVE FORWARD IS ...

- •

OTHER THOUGHTS ...

_____

_____

_____

_____

_____

TODAY, I'M GRATEFUL FOR ...

_____

_____

TODAY, I WILL STOP WORKING AT ...

_____ AM / PM

☀

6:00

7:00

8:00

9:00

10:00

11:00

12:00

1:00

2:00

3:00

4:00

5:00

6:00

7:00

8:00

☾

You're awesome! Go rock the day! 😊 👍 🚀 💥

TIME   PLACE   DATE

TODAY I FEEL
(C'MON, BE HONEST - CIRCLE ONE)

I FEEL THIS WAY BECAUSE ...

-
-
-

TO FEEL MORE ENERGIZED I CAN ...
(WHAT PEOPLE OR ACTIVITIES GIVE YOU A BOOST?)

TODAY, MY TOP PROJECT IS ...

THIS PROJECT MATTERS TO ME BECAUSE ...

-

ONE SMALL ACTION I CAN TAKE TO MOVE FORWARD IS ...

-

OTHER THOUGHTS ...

TODAY, I'M GRATEFUL FOR ...

TODAY, I WILL STOP WORKING AT ...

_____ AM / PM

☀

6:00

7:00

8:00

9:00

10:00

11:00

12:00

1:00

2:00

3:00

4:00

5:00

6:00

7:00

8:00

☾

You're awesome! Go rock the day! 😊 👍 🚀 💥

TODAY I FEEL
(C'MON, BE HONEST - CIRCLE ONE)

I FEEL THIS WAY BECAUSE ...

-
-
-

TO FEEL MORE ENERGIZED I CAN ...
(WHAT PEOPLE OR ACTIVITIES GIVE YOU A BOOST?)

TODAY, MY TOP PROJECT IS ...

THIS PROJECT MATTERS TO ME BECAUSE ...

-

ONE SMALL ACTION I CAN TAKE TO MOVE FORWARD IS ...

-

OTHER THOUGHTS ...

TODAY, I'M GRATEFUL FOR ...

TODAY, I WILL STOP WORKING AT ...

_____ AM / PM

NOTES — PLAN THE DAY — BRAIN DUMP
(FREE SPACE TO HELP FREE YOUR MIND)

☀

6:00

7:00

8:00

9:00

10:00

11:00

12:00

1:00

2:00

3:00

4:00

5:00

6:00

7:00

8:00

☾

You're awesome! Go rock the day! 😉 👍 🚀 💥

TODAY I FEEL
(C'MON, BE HONEST - CIRCLE ONE)

I FEEL THIS WAY BECAUSE ...

-
-
-

TO FEEL MORE ENERGIZED I CAN ...
(WHAT PEOPLE OR ACTIVITIES GIVE YOU A BOOST?)

TODAY, MY TOP PROJECT IS ...

THIS PROJECT MATTERS TO ME BECAUSE ...

-

ONE SMALL ACTION I CAN TAKE TO MOVE FORWARD IS ...

-

OTHER THOUGHTS ...

TODAY, I'M GRATEFUL FOR ...

TODAY, I WILL STOP WORKING AT ...

_____ AM / PM

☀

6:00

7:00

8:00

9:00

10:00

11:00

12:00

1:00

2:00

3:00

4:00

5:00

6:00

7:00

8:00

☾

You're awesome! Go rock the day! 😉 👍 🚀 💥

TODAY I FEEL
(C'MON, BE HONEST - CIRCLE ONE)

I FEEL THIS WAY BECAUSE …

-
-
-

TO FEEL MORE ENERGIZED I CAN …
(WHAT PEOPLE OR ACTIVITIES GIVE YOU A BOOST?)

TODAY, MY TOP PROJECT IS …

THIS PROJECT MATTERS TO ME BECAUSE …

-

ONE SMALL ACTION I CAN TAKE TO MOVE FORWARD IS …

-

OTHER THOUGHTS …

TODAY, I'M GRATEFUL FOR …

TODAY, I WILL STOP WORKING AT …

_____ AM / PM

NOTES — PLAN THE DAY — BRAIN DUMP
(FREE SPACE TO HELP FREE YOUR MIND)

☀

6:00

7:00

8:00

9:00

10:00

11:00

12:00

1:00

2:00

3:00

4:00

5:00

6:00

7:00

8:00

☾

You're awesome! Go rock the day! 😊 👍 🚀 💥

TODAY I FEEL
(C'MON, BE HONEST - CIRCLE ONE)

I FEEL THIS WAY BECAUSE ...

-
-
-

TO FEEL MORE ENERGIZED I CAN ...
(WHAT PEOPLE OR ACTIVITIES GIVE YOU A BOOST?)

TODAY, MY TOP PROJECT IS ...

THIS PROJECT MATTERS TO ME BECAUSE ...

-

ONE SMALL ACTION I CAN TAKE TO MOVE FORWARD IS ...

-

OTHER THOUGHTS ...

TODAY, I'M GRATEFUL FOR ...

TODAY, I WILL STOP WORKING AT ...

_____ AM / PM

☀

6:00

7:00

8:00

9:00

10:00

11:00

12:00

1:00

2:00

3:00

4:00

5:00

6:00

7:00

8:00

☾

You're awesome! Go rock the day! 😊 👍 🚀 💥

TODAY I FEEL
(C'MON, BE HONEST - CIRCLE ONE)

I FEEL THIS WAY BECAUSE ...

-
-
-

TO FEEL MORE ENERGIZED I CAN ...
(WHAT PEOPLE OR ACTIVITIES GIVE YOU A BOOST?)

TODAY, MY TOP PROJECT IS ...

THIS PROJECT MATTERS TO ME BECAUSE ...

-

ONE SMALL ACTION I CAN TAKE TO MOVE FORWARD IS ...

-

OTHER THOUGHTS ...

TODAY, I'M GRATEFUL FOR ...

TODAY, I WILL STOP WORKING AT ...

_____ AM / PM

NOTES — PLAN THE DAY — BRAIN DUMP
(FREE SPACE TO HELP FREE YOUR MIND)

☀

6:00

7:00

8:00

9:00

10:00

11:00

12:00

1:00

2:00

3:00

4:00

5:00

6:00

7:00

8:00

☾

You're awesome! Go rock the day! 😊 👍 🚀 💥

TODAY I FEEL
(C'MON, BE HONEST - CIRCLE ONE)

I FEEL THIS WAY BECAUSE ...

-
-
-

TO FEEL MORE ENERGIZED I CAN ...
(WHAT PEOPLE OR ACTIVITIES GIVE YOU A BOOST?)

TODAY, MY TOP PROJECT IS ...

THIS PROJECT MATTERS TO ME BECAUSE ...

-

ONE SMALL ACTION I CAN TAKE TO MOVE FORWARD IS ...

-

OTHER THOUGHTS ...

TODAY, I'M GRATEFUL FOR ...

TODAY, I WILL STOP WORKING AT ...

_____ AM / PM

☀

6:00

7:00

8:00

9:00

10:00

11:00

12:00

1:00

2:00

3:00

4:00

5:00

6:00

7:00

8:00

☾

You're awesome! Go rock the day! 😊 👍 🚀 💥

TODAY I FEEL
(C'MON, BE HONEST - CIRCLE ONE)

I FEEL THIS WAY BECAUSE ...

-
-
-

TO FEEL MORE ENERGIZED I CAN ...
(WHAT PEOPLE OR ACTIVITIES GIVE YOU A BOOST?)

TODAY, MY TOP PROJECT IS ...

THIS PROJECT MATTERS TO ME BECAUSE ...

-

ONE SMALL ACTION I CAN TAKE TO MOVE FORWARD IS ...

-

OTHER THOUGHTS ...

TODAY, I'M GRATEFUL FOR ...

TODAY, I WILL STOP WORKING AT ...

_____ AM / PM

NOTES — PLAN THE DAY — BRAIN DUMP

(FREE SPACE TO HELP FREE YOUR MIND)

☀

6:00

7:00

8:00

9:00

10:00

11:00

12:00

1:00

2:00

3:00

4:00

5:00

6:00

7:00

8:00

☾

You're awesome! Go rock the day! 😉 👍 🚀 💥

TODAY I FEEL
(C'MON, BE HONEST - CIRCLE ONE)

I FEEL THIS WAY BECAUSE ...

-
-
-

TO FEEL MORE ENERGIZED I CAN ...
(WHAT PEOPLE OR ACTIVITIES GIVE YOU A BOOST?)

TODAY, MY TOP PROJECT IS ...

THIS PROJECT MATTERS TO ME BECAUSE ...

-

ONE SMALL ACTION I CAN TAKE TO MOVE FORWARD IS ...

-

OTHER THOUGHTS ...

TODAY, I'M GRATEFUL FOR ...

TODAY, I WILL STOP WORKING AT ...

_____ AM / PM

☀

6:00

7:00

8:00

9:00

10:00

11:00

12:00

1:00

2:00

3:00

4:00

5:00

6:00

7:00

8:00

☾

You're awesome! Go rock the day! 😄 👍 🚀 💥

TODAY I FEEL
(C'MON, BE HONEST - CIRCLE ONE)

Depleted Meh Fine Good Energized

I FEEL THIS WAY BECAUSE ...

-
-
-

TO FEEL MORE ENERGIZED I CAN ...
(WHAT PEOPLE OR ACTIVITIES GIVE YOU A BOOST?)

TODAY, MY TOP PROJECT IS ...

THIS PROJECT MATTERS TO ME BECAUSE ...

-

ONE SMALL ACTION I CAN TAKE TO MOVE FORWARD IS ...

-

OTHER THOUGHTS ...

TODAY, I'M GRATEFUL FOR ...

TODAY, I WILL STOP WORKING AT ...

_____ AM / PM

NOTES — PLAN THE DAY — BRAIN DUMP
(FREE SPACE TO HELP FREE YOUR MIND)

☀

6:00

7:00

8:00

9:00

10:00

11:00

12:00

1:00

2:00

3:00

4:00

5:00

6:00

7:00

8:00

☾

You're awesome! Go rock the day! 😄 👍 🚀 💥

TODAY I FEEL
(C'MON, BE HONEST - CIRCLE ONE)

I FEEL THIS WAY BECAUSE ...

-
-
-

TO FEEL MORE ENERGIZED I CAN ...
(WHAT PEOPLE OR ACTIVITIES GIVE YOU A BOOST?)

TODAY, MY TOP PROJECT IS ...

THIS PROJECT MATTERS TO ME BECAUSE ...

-

ONE SMALL ACTION I CAN TAKE TO MOVE FORWARD IS ...

-

OTHER THOUGHTS ...

TODAY, I'M GRATEFUL FOR ...

TODAY, I WILL STOP WORKING AT ...

_____ AM / PM

NOTES — PLAN THE DAY — BRAIN DUMP
(FREE SPACE TO HELP FREE YOUR MIND)

☀

6:00

7:00

8:00

9:00

10:00

11:00

12:00

1:00

2:00

3:00

4:00

5:00

6:00

7:00

8:00

☾

You're awesome! Go rock the day! 😊 👍 🚀 💥

TODAY I FEEL
(C'MON, BE HONEST - CIRCLE ONE)

I FEEL THIS WAY BECAUSE ...

-
-
-

TO FEEL MORE ENERGIZED I CAN ...
(WHAT PEOPLE OR ACTIVITIES GIVE YOU A BOOST?)

TODAY, MY TOP PROJECT IS ...

THIS PROJECT MATTERS TO ME BECAUSE ...

-

ONE SMALL ACTION I CAN TAKE TO MOVE FORWARD IS ...

-

OTHER THOUGHTS ...

TODAY, I'M GRATEFUL FOR ...

TODAY, I WILL STOP WORKING AT ...

_____ AM / PM

☀

6:00

7:00

8:00

9:00

10:00

11:00

12:00

1:00

2:00

3:00

4:00

5:00

6:00

7:00

8:00

☾

You're awesome! Go rock the day! 😊 👍 🚀 💥

TODAY I FEEL
(C'MON, BE HONEST - CIRCLE ONE)

I FEEL THIS WAY BECAUSE ...

-
-
-

TO FEEL MORE ENERGIZED I CAN ...
(WHAT PEOPLE OR ACTIVITIES GIVE YOU A BOOST?)

TODAY, MY TOP PROJECT IS ...

THIS PROJECT MATTERS TO ME BECAUSE ...

-

ONE SMALL ACTION I CAN TAKE TO MOVE FORWARD IS ...

-

OTHER THOUGHTS ...

TODAY, I'M GRATEFUL FOR ...

TODAY, I WILL STOP WORKING AT ...

_____ AM / PM

NOTES — PLAN THE DAY — BRAIN DUMP

(FREE SPACE TO HELP FREE YOUR MIND)

☀

6:00

7:00

8:00

9:00

10:00

11:00

12:00

1:00

2:00

3:00

4:00

5:00

6:00

7:00

8:00

☾

You're awesome! Go rock the day! 😌 👍 🚀 💥

TODAY I FEEL
(C'MON, BE HONEST - CIRCLE ONE)

I FEEL THIS WAY BECAUSE ...

-
-
-

TO FEEL MORE ENERGIZED I CAN ...
(WHAT PEOPLE OR ACTIVITIES GIVE YOU A BOOST?)

TODAY, MY TOP PROJECT IS ...

THIS PROJECT MATTERS TO ME BECAUSE ...

-

ONE SMALL ACTION I CAN TAKE TO MOVE FORWARD IS ...

-

OTHER THOUGHTS ...

TODAY, I'M GRATEFUL FOR ...

TODAY, I WILL STOP WORKING AT ...

_____ AM / PM

☀

6:00

7:00

8:00

9:00

10:00

11:00

12:00

1:00

2:00

3:00

4:00

5:00

6:00

7:00

8:00

☾

You're awesome! Go rock the day! 😊 👍 🚀 💥

TIME   📍 PLACE   DATE

TODAY I FEEL
(C'MON, BE HONEST - CIRCLE ONE)

I FEEL THIS WAY BECAUSE ...

-
-
-

TO FEEL MORE ENERGIZED I CAN ...
(WHAT PEOPLE OR ACTIVITIES GIVE YOU A BOOST?)

_____

_____

TODAY, MY TOP PROJECT IS ...

_____

_____

THIS PROJECT MATTERS TO ME BECAUSE ...

-

ONE SMALL ACTION I CAN TAKE TO MOVE FORWARD IS ...

-

OTHER THOUGHTS ...

_____

_____

_____

_____

_____

TODAY, I'M GRATEFUL FOR ...

_____

_____

TODAY, I WILL STOP WORKING AT ...

_____ AM / PM

NOTES — PLAN THE DAY — BRAIN DUMP
(FREE SPACE TO HELP FREE YOUR MIND)

☀

6:00

7:00

8:00

9:00

10:00

11:00

12:00

1:00

2:00

3:00

4:00

5:00

6:00

7:00

8:00

☾

You're awesome! Go rock the day! 😊 👍 🚀 💥

TODAY I FEEL
(C'MON, BE HONEST - CIRCLE ONE)

I FEEL THIS WAY BECAUSE ...

-
-
-

TO FEEL MORE ENERGIZED I CAN ...
(WHAT PEOPLE OR ACTIVITIES GIVE YOU A BOOST?)

TODAY, MY TOP PROJECT IS ...

THIS PROJECT MATTERS TO ME BECAUSE ...

-

ONE SMALL ACTION I CAN TAKE TO MOVE FORWARD IS ...

-

OTHER THOUGHTS ...

TODAY, I'M GRATEFUL FOR ...

TODAY, I WILL STOP WORKING AT ...

_____ AM / PM

☀

6:00

7:00

8:00

9:00

10:00

11:00

12:00

1:00

2:00

3:00

4:00

5:00

6:00

7:00

8:00

☾

You're awesome! Go rock the day! 😊👍🚀💥

TIME   📍 PLACE   DATE

TODAY I FEEL
(C'MON, BE HONEST - CIRCLE ONE)

I FEEL THIS WAY BECAUSE …

-
-
-

TO FEEL MORE ENERGIZED I CAN …
(WHAT PEOPLE OR ACTIVITIES GIVE YOU A BOOST?)

TODAY, MY TOP PROJECT IS …

THIS PROJECT MATTERS TO ME BECAUSE …

-

ONE SMALL ACTION I CAN TAKE TO MOVE FORWARD IS …

-

OTHER THOUGHTS …

TODAY, I'M GRATEFUL FOR …

TODAY, I WILL STOP WORKING AT …

_____ AM / PM

☀

6:00

7:00

8:00

9:00

10:00

11:00

12:00

1:00

2:00

3:00

4:00

5:00

6:00

7:00

8:00

☾

You're awesome! Go rock the day! 😌 👍 🚀 💥

TODAY I FEEL
(C'MON, BE HONEST - CIRCLE ONE)

I FEEL THIS WAY BECAUSE ...

-
-
-

TO FEEL MORE ENERGIZED I CAN ...
(WHAT PEOPLE OR ACTIVITIES GIVE YOU A BOOST?)

TODAY, MY TOP PROJECT IS ...

THIS PROJECT MATTERS TO ME BECAUSE ...

-

ONE SMALL ACTION I CAN TAKE TO MOVE FORWARD IS ...

-

OTHER THOUGHTS ...

TODAY, I'M GRATEFUL FOR ...

TODAY, I WILL STOP WORKING AT ...

_____ AM / PM

☀

6:00

7:00

8:00

9:00

10:00

11:00

12:00

1:00

2:00

3:00

4:00

5:00

6:00

7:00

8:00

☾

You're awesome! Go rock the day! 😊 👍 🚀 💥

TODAY I FEEL
(C'MON, BE HONEST - CIRCLE ONE)

I FEEL THIS WAY BECAUSE ...

-
-
-

TO FEEL MORE ENERGIZED I CAN ...
(WHAT PEOPLE OR ACTIVITIES GIVE YOU A BOOST?)

TODAY, MY TOP PROJECT IS ...

THIS PROJECT MATTERS TO ME BECAUSE ...

-

ONE SMALL ACTION I CAN TAKE TO MOVE FORWARD IS ...

-

OTHER THOUGHTS ...

TODAY, I'M GRATEFUL FOR ...

TODAY, I WILL STOP WORKING AT ...

_____ AM / PM

NOTES — PLAN THE DAY — BRAIN DUMP
(FREE SPACE TO HELP FREE YOUR MIND)

☀

6:00

7:00

8:00

9:00

10:00

11:00

12:00

1:00

2:00

3:00

4:00

5:00

6:00

7:00

8:00

☾

You're awesome! Go rock the day! 😊 👍 🚀 💥

PROJECT AWESOME

This may be the end of your *5 Second Journal*, but it's far from the end of your journey. You're just starting to discover the Awesome that lives inside you, and I want to help you strengthen that.

Now that you've learned to 5-4-3-2-1 get sh*t done, I invite you to be part of a growing online movement designed to connect you with the tools and support you need to step into your Awesome every day.

What's this amazing movement called? Project Awesome, of course!

P.S. TO LEARN MORE GO TO ...
www.melrobbins.com/ProjectAwesome